ERASING SCARS

Herpes and Healing

— — — — — ❧❧❦❦ — — — — —

James D. Okun, M.D.
and
Evangelita Goodwell, O.A.A.C.

ERASING SCARS: HERPES AND HEALING
Copyright © 2016, 1997 by James D. Okun.
All rights reserved.

We dedicate this book to Eli Siegel and to our children Charlie, Jane, and Jeremy, because without the beautiful good will of Eli Siegel these children would have never been born and we would never have worked together to have things known.

We are grateful to our editor, Ed Roberts, for the title to this book and for his professional editing and assistance in making this book possible. We also want to thank Charles Wenk for believing enough in this project to help raise it off the ground.

CONTENTS

INTRODUCTION

My education and training were fairly conventional up until 1985. I graduated from Glen Cove High School on Long Island in New York and went on to attend Duke University for my premedical education, graduating from there Phi Beta Kappa in 1978. Early in my studies at Duke, I became interested in the effects of stress on the body and discovered during my freshman year the work of Dr. Edmund Jacobson, who had developed therapies and techniques for Progressive Relaxation after his studies at Harvard. I became so interested in Dr. Jacobson's work that I visited him at his laboratory in Chicago to study with him, returning to Duke to found the Duke University Center for Tension Control in order to help my fellow students deal with stress, which was certainly high among the highly motivated and competitive Duke students. The organization sponsored many workshops for students and brought in outside speakers who specialized in stress reduction. I supplemented my studies of stress by taking an engineering class with Dr. John Artley, who had a special interest in biofeedback; during the course I participated in research projects dealing with the effects of biofeedback in treating stress and disease.

After graduating from Duke, I attended the Albert Einstein College of Medicine, Bronx, New York, where again, as time permitted, I began to delve into alternative therapies such as hypnosis and to study the importance of a patient's cultural background in terms of both physical and mental illness. In my fourth year of medical school, I had the opportunity to study acupuncture while taking a neurology elective course from Boston University Hospital. I went on to spend the last six weeks of medical school in London at the Moorfields Eye Hospital, where I was exposed to British views on eye disease and preventive medicine. At the end of my training, I went into my internship at Framingham Union Hospital in Framingham, Massachusetts, home of the famous Framingham Heart studies. At Framingham, I and my colleagues were exposed to the latest views on preventive medicine, as Framingham at the time was a mecca for these studies.

It was at this time that my own health suddenly became an issue, and my interest in alternative medicine was sharply revived. I had been accepted by and felt very honored to be in training in ophthalmology at the prestigious Ochsner Foundation Hospital in New Orleans, under the direction of Tom Zimmerman, the inventor of the Timoptic eye drop, a revolutionary advance in the treatment of glaucoma. Ophthalmology as a discipline itself requires great acuity of vision, perhaps the most acute vision possible for any medical specialty. Before my arrival at Ochsner, I was diagnosed with keratoconus, a progressive disease of the cornea in which the cornea gradually thins and often perforates. The only known treatment at the time for keratoconus was a prescription of rigid contact lenses, until such time as the vision deteriorated so much as to require a corneal transplant in one or both eyes.

As the time drew near for me to begin my ophthalmology residency, I began to panic, not only from the stress and sleeplessness that came with being an intern, but also because I could not get fitted with a pair of contacts that I could see out of or which I could wear comfortably. I went to a Harvard specialist, the inventor of the Boston Lens, who was supposed to be such a wizard with contact lens prescriptions, but I left his office in tears because the lens hurt so much and I still couldn't see properly. My anxiety over my studies in ophthalmology grew, and I again embarked on a search for relief and help from alternative practices. I went on to try acupuncture, palming of the eyes for relaxation, meditation, and other exotic forms of therapy. One of these was a stint with Dr. Leslie Salov of White Water, Wisconsin, formerly a high-powered ophthalmologist and eye surgeon, who was then almost blind himself from macular degeneration. He had found no help from traditional medicine, so he'd developed a program for treating eye disease consisting of a study of nutrition, anatomy, and the effects of light and radiation, supplemented with studies of religion and miracles and a regimen of exercise, walking, and sunning, all in a farm-like setting for a two-week period and a cost of about five thousand dollars. Some of what I got from my studies at Dr. Salov's was in harmony with what I'd learned back at Duke about Transactional Analysis, while other aspects of Dr. Salov's program hearkened back to things I'd heard about back at Einstein.

But after one year, in 1985, with the unfortunate encouragement of my parents, I decided to leave the ophthalmology residency program at Ochsner. It was at this low point that I intensified my search for something that would finally help my eyesight and the genital herpes that I had contracted back in 1982 while in medical school.

I began to devote my days to stretching, working out with a personal trainer, following a diet of totally organic foods, and investigating other alternative practices. I took up crystal therapy, tai-chi, massage therapy, zero balancing, visualization and imaging techniques; I visited mud baths and flotation tanks in California, went through more biofeedback, tried chiropractic adjustments, and submitted myself to many different types of New Age body work, including Rolfing.

As I was on my way out of the ophthalmology residency program, though, I had met the beautiful young woman who later became my wife and the mother of our sons Charlie and Jeremy and our beautiful daughter Jane, and during the course of getting to know her, she introduced me to a philosophy that she had discovered when in her late teens and which she had been studying for over twenty years. The philosophy is called Aesthetic Realism and was developed by the poet and critic Eli Siegel beginning with his award-winning poem "Hot Afternoons Have Been in Montana" in 1924 (and ending with his death in 1978). With all of the training I'd had and with all of the searching I'd done, I was at first skeptical that here, finally, was what I had been searching for for so long. After thousands of dollars in expenses and travels around the country in search of real help, here was something that had been right under my nose when I had been studying in New York; but I hadn't heard of it—it had been ignored or made fun of during the course of the previous four decades. I couldn't believe it at first—but here it was.

My wife told me that she had seen Aesthetic Realism work with students with a wide variety of ailments—migraines, seizures, digestive problems, stuttering, for instance; it had even been instrumental in over a hundred men "changing" from homosexuality. She told me that she didn't know whether Aesthetic Realism could be of any help with either keratoconus

4

or herpes, but she confided that it was something that had saved her life and made her whole, and she wondered whether it could do the same for me.

I felt that I had nothing to lose; nothing else that I'd tried had helped in any significant way. I began to study aesthetics, which taught me that the structure of the world and of myself is aesthetic, as are my everyday problems. There are aesthetic solutions to disease, I learned, and I discovered that what I was trying to do was to put together opposites in myself; and everything else that I had studied seemed to fall beautifully into place. As things fell more and more into place, as everything I had studied began to take on a much deeper integrity, my corneas tightened up, becoming flatter and flatter until my vision became better and better. As I studied Aesthetic Realism, I discovered the link between deep psychological pain and its relation to both my vision problem and my herpes infection. In due course, I became able to drive and work with good sight, not only with contacts but with glasses (which is unheard of in cases of keratoconus). My corneas eventually became entirely normal, with my vision crystal clear in contact lenses and in glasses. I attribute this medical miracle to the release from and the lessening of internal stress and pain, which I attribute to the former views that I held, an inaccurate and contemptuous way of viewing the world that Aesthetic Realism laid bare. And not only was my keratoconus dealt with successfully, but through my studies of Aesthetic Realism, I was able to determine the cause of my herpes outbreaks and since this discovery, I have been entirely free of herpes outbreaks—not only that, but my wife never contracted the virus, and our baby girl was born alive and healthy, not dead or deformed.

ERASING SCARS

Over the years since I was introduced to Aesthetic Realism, my wife and I have worked with over fifty patients with genital herpes, one of them with severe herpes scarring on the face, and every one of them, just like me, has been able to determine the cause of his outbreaks.

As a physician who has himself suffered the debilitating effects of herpes attacks, I feel obliged to share what I have learned for the benefit of other sufferers. My willingness to share this news has earned me the ire of many in the medical establishment, however; the Louisiana State Medical Board moved to suspend my license, for example. I am convinced, though, that Aesthetic Realism teaches people an accurate way of dealing with the stresses inherent to life, and its role in alleviating stress, I am convinced, is directly connected with the body's own immune responses, such as are called into play in fighting the herpes virus.

CHAPTER 1:
The Psychobioimmunology of Herpes Virus Infections

Herpes viruses infect the human being of every race, in every country, and in every part of the world. Infection with Herpes Simplex Virus Type I (HSV I) or Herpes Simplex Virus Type II (HSV II) viruses devastates millions of patients around the world without regard to race, color, creed, gender, or income or education level. It is estimated that in this country alone there are at least forty million Americans infected with Genital Herpes, with 500,000 new cases being reported each year,[1] and approximately one hundred million patients infected with both HSV I and HSV II in the United States, according to statistics from the Burroughs Wellcome Company's Research Division.

According to statistics from the Centers for Disease Control and Prevention in Atlanta (CDC),[2] initial visits to physicians' offices in the United States for Genital Herpes infections, between the years 1966 and 1993, rose from approximately 15,000 in 1966 to approximately 175,000 in 1993, with a peak of approximately 230,000 initial patient visits to physicians' offices for Genital Herpes Simplex virus infections in 1990.

Here, I will summarize the current state of knowledge about HSV infections and will attempt to update the public on the newest advances in a relatively new area of research now called "psychobioimmunology," "psychoneuroimmunology," or "neuroimmunomodulation"—all three terms refer to a new discipline that deals with the relation of stress to disease and the effect of various stresses on the immune system and the body's ability to fight off disease.

Herpes Simplex Virus Types I and II, which are members of the "Herpes Virus Hominis" family, cause many different diseases in human beings. These include gingivostomatitis, herpes keratitis of the cornea, herpes labialis (cold sores), and herpes infections of the male genitalia.

The herpes virus particle is made up of protein, DNA, lipid, and carbohydrates. In general, there are twenty-five parts carbohydrate to one hundred parts DNA and 320 parts phospho-lipid for every one hundred parts of protein. The herpes virus DNA is what is known as double-stranded DNA, with a molecular weight of the virus particle of approximately 100×106 daltons. Research has determined that the herpes virus particle is made up of a central core measuring approximately 75 nm in diameter with a capsid measuring approximately 100 nm in diameter.

The shape of the herpes virus particle is of an icosahedron, usually with a surrounding envelope (which is derived from the host cell membrane) and measures 145 to 200 nm. Herpes virus particles may appear either with or without envelopes and with or without cores. Both "naked" and "enveloped" viral particles are capable of infecting cells. After the initiation of infection, absorption is completed within three hours. The DNA of the virus enters the nucleus of the infected cell and takes over the DNA replication machinery to synthesize new virus DNA utilizing the replication machinery of the infected cell. Viral proteins are synthesized in the cytoplasm of the infected cell and are transported to the nucleus.

The new virus particle typically has a three-layered envelope. The innermost part of the envelope is produced within the nucleus, while the second part of the envelope is produced at the nuclear membrane and the third at the cytoplasmic membrane. Most of the envelope is made up of material from the host. It is estimated that an infected cell may produce up to one thousand virus particles with only five to ten percent of these being infectious.

After initial exposure to the Herpes Simplex Virus, humoral antibodies appear in the bloodstream. It is thought that various polypeptides of the virus capsid stimulate the production of these antibodies. IGM antibodies are the first to appear after initial exposure to the virus and usually appear within one week after exposure. IGG antibodies usually appear one week after the initial infection as the synthesis of the IGM antibodies begins to decrease.

It is thought that cellular immunity is also stimulated by the invading herpes virus and may actually be of greater importance in inhibiting the replication of the virus particles and the relapsing from remission into a herpes virus infection and outbreak. The average incubation period is between two and twelve days after initial infection. Normally, infection occurs after contact with infected moist mucous membranes.

Upon initial infection through a susceptible skin cell, the herpes virus enters a cell, replicates, and then travels along the nerve to a nerve ganglion or collection of nerve cells where it lies in remission until reactivation. The initial infection may be characterized by reddening of the skin and prodromal symptoms which include vague deep pains, a feeling of itching and burning, fatigue, and flu-like symptoms. (Asymptomatic viral shedding may precede the initial symptoms, and so a patient may indeed be infectious although he has not yet had a clinically significant outbreak.)

After the initial prodromal symptoms, including pain and flu-like symptoms (or sometimes not preceded by any symptoms at all), the overlying skin may become reddened as a first-stage preliminary to the eruption of the grouped vesicles. The vesicles or blisters contain clear fluid. When the vesicles are unroofed and cultured, only viral particles and no bacteria can be isolated. A Tzanck prep of these vesicles will show the characteristic giant cells which are diagnostic of HSV infection.

Oftentimes, the lesions will become ulcerated and extremely painful, preventing healing, especially if the lesions are located in a skinfold where healing is more difficult (the vesicles may inadvertently become unroofed as the area where the vesicles are brushes against clothing, causing excruciating pain). After the lesions crust over (usually within seven to ten days), the virus will then remain quiescent within the ganglion, only intermittently releasing virus along the nerve fibers, until the time when something stimulates the viruses to re-awaken and reproduce and to rise out of the ganglion to travel, once again, along the same nerve pathway originally traversed during the initial outbreak. The viruses follow this nerve pathway back to the site of initial infection where they once again cause erythema and the eruption of the excruciatingly painful blisters.

HSV infections multiply in many different human tissues (including lymphocytes), and since they reproduce and hide inside cells, the infections have the ability to escape antibodies produced against the virus. Since the advent of the polio vaccine and the eradication of the polio virus, the Herpes Virus has become the most frequent cause of viral encephalitis in the United States, with HSV II becoming a common sexually transmitted disease, more common than such diseases as syphilis, hepatitis B (sexually transmitted), and AIDS, according to incidence figures from the CDC.[3]

It is also of note that women who are infected with HSV II have a higher incidence of cancer of the cervix and that women who have active herpes lesions during their third trimester face an extremely high risk of fetal death due to the deadly effect of neonatal herpes. Infants who contract neonatal herpes have about a fifty percent mortality rate if they contract herpes from the mother's active lesions in the birth canal. Neonates simply cannot tolerate the insult of the herpes infection, and most succumb to neonatal sepsis and death.

In herpes encephalitis, there occurs (for reasons that are poorly understood) an ascent of the HSV I infection from the nose through the olfactory tract up to the frontal and temporal lobes of the brain. There have been estimates that up to thirty-eight percent of patients who are in a coma from herpes encephalitis and who have seizures or paralysis will die, with any survivors having severe neurologic impairment.

Herpes encephalitis can affect persons of any age, sex, race, or economic status. About fifteen percent of patients who develop herpes encephalitis have histories of recurrent Herpes Labialis.

Patients in these cases become acutely sick several days before they are admitted to the hospital. Patients experience headache, sore throat, fever, nausea, vomiting, nasal congestion, and sometimes photophobia, vertigo, insomnia, and anorexia. One-third of the patients will develop concurrent fever blisters during the course of their illness. Other patients will become paralyzed or comatose.

It is recognized worldwide that the treatment of choice for HSV infections is Zovirax or Acyclovir. Acyclovir terminates herpes DNA chains completely and after incorporation. Since Zovirax is highly selective, it leaves healthy cells virtually unaffected while providing powerful inhibitions even at low intracellular concentrations. In a study from Goldberg et al.[4] and a placebo-controlled study by Meartz et al.,[5] patients were studied over a six-year period to determine the efficacy of Zovirax as suppressive therapy to reduce the mean number of recurrences. This study clearly showed a dramatic reduction in the mean number of recurrences. The CDC treatment guidelines support the use of Zovirax 200 mg. five times a day for five days for patients with frequent or severe recurrences. The CDC maintains that suppressive therapy reduces the frequency of recurrences by at least seventy-five percent.

What is the meaning of stress? To accurately and adequately describe it, we must note that the sympathetic nervous system is the physical structure in human beings that provides for the physiologic ability to mobilize the physical body to flee in an emergency. When someone perceives a threat, the hypothalamic-pituitary axis takes over normal functioning. Adrenaline and other catecholamines are released into the bloodstream. This action leads to the effects commonly seen when one is frightened: the pupils dilate, the heart rate speeds up, respiration increases, and the body mobilizes for the emergency at hand.

Psychobioimmunology has gained popularity recently as research continues to document the effect on the body and the immune system of various stresses. Glaser and Glaser have actually documented decreases in peripheral lymphocytes in patients under stress. As the lymphocytes decrease, so does the ability to fight off disease. Kemeny and Cohen[6] have studied the relationship between stress and depression and genital herpes outbreaks. They have documented the lowering of both CD4 (+) helper-inducer and CD8 (+) suppressor-cytotoxic t-cells in patients with high-stress levels and decreased CD8 (+) cells in patients with high-stress levels and decreased CD8 (+) cells in patients with high levels of depression. Patients who were severely depressed were found to have higher rates of HSV outbreaks.

Bierman, a dermatologist from UCLA, has written extensively on the importance of understanding the psychological implications of being infected with the herpes virus.[7] He describes a scenario of shame, guilt, and anger along with depression and a feeling of hopelessness that accompanies an outbreak. He makes the point that if a doctor does not make a heartfelt attempt to put the patient at ease in terms of understanding his infection, a vicious cycle will ensue in which the patient will not improve but indeed will deteriorate because the patient does not understand the pathology of his infection.

I have conducted clinical research exactly along these same lines, utilizing a basically unknown theory concerning self and disease postulated by Eli Siegel in the 1940s. Siegel has written extensively on the concept of disease interpreted as being "lack of ease."[8] He has proposed what this author believes to be revolutionary new concepts in the understanding and treatment of disease, and these concepts center around the need to understand how stress is directly related to one's perception of one's environment. Siegel points out that nervousness or anxiety is directly due to the desire to boost oneself up and give oneself false importance by making less of everything else; this is what Siegel defines as the dangerous tendency for "contempt," which is the ultimate cause of mental and psychosomatic disorders.[9]

I have worked with patients with both HSV I and HSV II who seek to know how they can avoid further outbreaks. Many of these patients were on Zovirax, but they have acknowledged the need for something beyond solely pharmacological treatment of herpes infection. Using concepts derived from Aesthetic Realism as propounded by Siegel, I have been able to help these patients understand the causative factors leading to outbreaks. As they tracked these factors down and became aware of the forces working in them to their detriment, they were able to eliminate recurrences and outbreaks with greater effect. These concepts, which have been submitted to the NIH Department for Alternative Medicine complement the work of Dr. Bierman, who has dissected the psychological reaction of patients to their herpes infections.

Bierman has noted reactions that include "initial shock," "emotional numbing," a "frantic search for a cure," a "sense of isolation," concern about the ability to have relationships (especially sexual relationships), and tremendous anger and rage against the person that the patient perceives is responsible for his infection. Bierman has analyzed further the fear of the patient concerning the consequences of his HSV infection, including the possibility of infecting others, the threat of never being able to be a father or to give birth to children, and the risk for women of developing cervical cancer, since once infected with HSV they have a statistically greater chance of developing cervical cancer.

Dr. Bierman further discusses other psychological reactions to HSV infection, including fear, shame and guilt, which act to intensify a patient's social isolation and which may even lead the patient to practice celibacy. Bierman describes depression, helplessness, hopelessness, and even active suicidal ideation, which may ensue especially as the disease progresses and as outbreaks become more severe and frequent.

Bierman has described how the infected herpes patient may reactivate underlying psychopathology and also may further disorganize coping mechanisms which are already inadequate. He has also described what he calls the "herpes syndrome," the patient's psychologic reaction to HSV infection, characterized as a pervasive and almost obsessional concern over having herpes that totally takes over the patient's concerns during waking hours—every moment the patient seems concerned with the avoidance of an outbreak or with the pain of the current outbreak and what he can do to feel better.

Bierman describes what he has observed as a dermatologist in Los Angeles treating many patients infected with the herpes simplex virus. He describes their lowered self-esteem and is very insightful in picking up on the shame and guilt that every patient feels following the acquisition of HSV. He notes the inordinate frustration of many patients over "the failure of treatment." In addition, he notes the fear of the patient of never being able to return to the "normal" sexual activity that the patient had before being infected with the HSV virus.

Bierman has documented the "continuous, unpleasant intrusion into moments of quiet reverie of the infected herpes patient." He discusses the problems that ensue for the herpes sufferer in terms of any possible sexual relations with a potential sexual partner due to his fear of spreading the herpes infection to this person. Bierman also discusses the fact that "their real or imagined concerns leads to withdrawal from establishing relations," and finally he observes that the HSV patient often believes that he has been infected as a "penalty for real or imagined transgressions."

In his Presidential Address to the Los Angeles Dermatological Society on the subject of stress and the immune system,[10] Bierman discussed the importance of the immune system in fighting the invasion of the herpes virus. He talked about the "first line of defense" against infection being the skin and mucous membranes. He described how disruption of this barrier resulted in "signals [being] sent to the immune system by chemical mediators and then white blood cells [being] alerted," "hundreds of thousands of cells ... marshalled by a specific signal from the skin ... are attracted to the local site or sites where they can render aid and defense to the host."

Bierman went on to describe the crucial link between the brain and hypothalamus and the control of immune function. He spoke about the network of autonomic nerve endings located in the anterior hypothalamus at the base of the brain. (The hypothalamus is where neurohormones are produced which are known to control the peripheral white blood cells. New evidence shows that in response to stress, the hypothalamus can trigger the release of certain neurohormones or "send neural messages to special end organs." The hypothalamus may directly stimulate the adrenal gland or can directly affect the function of the t-cell.)

Bierman went on in his address to report a "psychoneuroimmunologic axis in which ... strong emotional disturbances in individuals is often accompanied by measurable immunologic abnormalities" and "peripheral t-cells have receptor sites for these brain neurohormones and neurotransmitters which when activated retard or hinder the capacity of these cells to fight infection."

> Once relegated to faith healers and practitioners of folk medicine, the idea that the conscious mind can influence the onset and outcome of various diseases is now widely accepted by the medical community. The central premise of this theory suggests that emotional stress may increase vulnerability to infection through operatives in the brain which impact on immune functions.

ERASING SCARS

Bierman summarized at the end of his presidential address:

It then appears that the best means for enhancing natural immunity is to concentrate and direct attention to personal stress. It would be naive and simplistic to assert that a change in emotional temperament will prevent infection and/or cancer. It is not, however, unrealistic to suggest that by diminishing life stresses the body can better function to deal with these matters, no longer encumbered by the immune suppressive influence of stress.

Notes

1. "Wellcome Dialog," page 1. © 1992 Burroughs Wellcome Co.

2, 3. CDC. Estimated incidence and prevalence statistics on HSV infection, 1995. Unpublished.

4. Goldberg, L. H., et al. 1993. Long-term suppression of recurrent genital herpes with acylovir. *Archives of Dermatology* 1229: 582.

5. Meartz, G. J., C. C. Jones, J. Mills, et al. 1988. Long-term acyclovir suppression of frequently recurring genital herpes simplex virus infection: A multicenter double-blind trial. *JAMA* 260: 201-6.

6. Kemeny, Margaret E., and Frances Cohen. 1989. Psychological and immunological predictors of genital her pes recurrence. *Psychosomatic Medicine* 51: 195-208.

7. Bierman, Stanley M. Focus Session #662. Genital herpes simplex infection: Pathophysiology, psychosocial and legal considerations.

8. Siegel, E. 1981. Philosophy of self and disease. In *Self and World,* 318. New York: Definition Press.

9. Siegel, E. 1981. Preface: Contempt causes insanity. In *Self and World,* 7, 8. New York: Definition Press.

10. Bierman, Stanley M. Stress induced modulation of the immune function. Presidential Address to Los Angeles Dermatological Society. Reprinted in 1990 from the Bierman Dermatology Newsletter.

CHAPTER 2:
Transcript of a Consultation Session with Steve

T he transcript that follows is a record of a two-hour conversation that we had with Steve on 2 February 1994. When Fred Reno of WBRZ-TV in Baton Rouge reviewed the video tape of this conversation, he commented, "What a powerful story ... it needs to be told." As will become clear with the reading of this transcript, our consultation with Steve helped him save his health; helped him see himself, his family and the world with a clearer understanding; helped him get back to work—in short, helped him save his life.

This interview indicates that Aesthetic Realism has a profound role to play in the control of herpes outbreaks. What Steve was able to accomplish has been achieved by numerous other patients as well.

James Okun, M.D., and
Evangelita Goodwell, O.A.A.C.
2 February 1994

Dr. Okun:
You have been using the cream, you said.

ERASING SCARS

Steve:
The cream, and I use the orals. It has been a while, but the orals, I find that very effective.

Dr. Okun:
And how often were you taking that?

Steve:
Three times a day. Three times a day, plus my whole face was covered with the salve, and like I said, I was getting a tube this big.

Dr. Okun:
A big 60-gram tube.

Steve:
It was huge. I mean, I had to use it sparingly. It was free, so I could really cake it on, and it got rid of it, fairly quick.

Dr. Okun:
Just to summarize what we talked about: you first got this about four years ago, if I remember right. You were in the Marine Corps, you were at Pendleton.

Steve:
I was in boot camp at the time in 1988. I had my first outbreak about four weeks into the boot camp.

Dr. Okun:
The first time you ever had an outbreak?

Steve:
Right, all of a sudden, I started getting these lesions and like, little miniature lacerations, just started leaking fluid.

Dr. Okun:
Were they all over your face?

Steve:
Right. They started all around here, on the chin, and I guess I touched my face, because it was itching, it spread all around here a little bit on my forehead and like huge sores, I mean from nowhere, I did not know what it was. I knew it wasn't acne.

Dr. Okun:
Right.

Steve:
I was done with the acne days.

Dr. Okun:
That is right, how old were you?

Steve:
I was nineteen at the time. It was more to it than acne.

Dr. Okun:
When you would get the attack, how long would it last, about?

Steve:
Oh, it lasted a few weeks, until I got the medication.

Dr. Okun:
And then it would kind of crust over.

Steve:
The medication really put a stop to it from getting worse. It kind of stayed the same for a while. He said it would stay the

same for a while, just be patient, and he had me scrub it with that little sponge. He said scrub it real hard and break all that crust off and the scabs, and it was like, gross. He said scrub it. It really hurt.

Dr. Okun:
The blisters would come out and then they would scab over.

Steve:
Right. It would leak and get really hard and crusty, he said just scrub all that off and just put on the topical solution. It really helped. It got rid of it pretty quick. But I can't afford that now.

Dr. Okun:
Whoa! When you first got it, how often would you get the outbreaks?

Steve:
After that first, initial one?

Dr. Okun:
Right.

Steve:
I'd say about, about a year, maybe a little less than a year, I went to Okinawa after that and had a small outbreak there around my mouth, on my lip, my chin and I had my record book. I did the same procedure, it took a little while, but I got rid of it.

Dr. Okun:
Is this very painful when you get this? Do you get them inside your mouth?

Steve:
Oh, no. Never inside, like right now, I have one coming out of my mouth. I mean it gets hard.

Dr. Okun:
Right.

Steve:
It catches on my skin and it hurts. And it is, like numb. A numb-like tingling sensation, and eventually it will be a sore.

Dr. Okun:
Do they get kind of ulcerated and deep? You said they just kind of weep.

Steve:
I never had it as bad as that first one. The first time I thought my face would have pot holes in it, and he told me don't worry about it, they don't leave scars; he said if anything, it will leave like a little pink, like a pink coloration, and I have a little bit of pink around here, and that never goes away, like if I can touch it right now, the ones I had years ago, it still has that little numb feeling, at all times, so more or less I really never got rid of it.

Dr. Okun:
Do you start feeling like you have the flu? You feel sick before you get it, or while you're getting it, do you feel feverish or sick?

Steve:
Never have.

Dr. Okun:
Body aches?

Steve:
I remember talking about that, but I never had anything like that. It, just out of the blue, that first time I had it. And I can spot them. I can tell whenever it is not a zit coming out, and I can spot it like that, and I know it is going to start spreading and coming out again.

Dr. Okun:
Did they tell you much about the virus?

Steve:
Not really, they just told me that it is Simplex I, Zolice.

Dr. Okun:
Zoster.

Steve:
They told me I would never get rid of it, it is in my blood for the rest of my life. And I could just take the Zovirax, cream and the orals, and it would just temporarily diminish, and that's about it.

Dr. Okun:
Do you put the cream on every day, four or five times a day?

Steve:
Oh, at least. Oh, at least. They did not want me to drink out of nobody else's canteen.

Dr. Okun:
Are you still in the service?

Steve:

Oh, no. They did not want me to share forks, anything like that. Quite embarrassing.

Dr. Okun:

What is the most embarrassing thing about it?

Steve:

I am embarrassed with it now. I don't really care to go into public too much because everybody says, man, what is on your face, and you don't really want to come out and say, well, I have Herpes, or whatever, everybody thinks it's like, whoa, something similar to AIDS whatever, it is not good for social life either, with women, that is.

Dr. Okun:

This attack, you say you've had for how long?

Steve:

It has been a while. I just didn't have the money and couldn't afford to get the medication.

Dr. Okun:

How much is a tube of that cream?

Steve:

$34.00 dollars for that tube.

Dr. Okun:

And the pills are very expensive, too?

Steve:

The pills are expensive, but they work.

Dr. Okun:
What I am going to do is go into a little bit about how the virus works, and show you some pictures, and we are going to go into some questions. Basically, it is the Herpes Simplex Virus. There is the Herpes I, which is above the belt, which is the best way to think about it, and Herpes II, below the belt, which is Genital Herpes. And the way it works is, when you get infected with it, the Herpes Virus attaches to your skin, it can be anywhere on the skin really. The virus attaches, and what it does is it actually injects its DNA into your skin cell, and infects your cell, and it actually takes over the genetic machinery of your skin cell and has it reproducing its own DNA, to make new virus particles. The first time you got infected, it attached to your skin cell, it injected its DNA, it started reproducing, and then what happens is the virus travels down the nerves leading from your skin to what they call the ganglion, which is a collection of nerve cells, where all the nerve cells are together. And that is where it lives, and that is where it sleeps. So what happens is, every time that you get a reactivation of the infection, the virus wakes up and travels back along the same path of the nerves, exactly to where ...

Steve:
The outbreak occurs.

Dr. Okun:
Right, do you find it is in the same place?

Steve:
Where it started from, yeah, basically the same place.

Dr. Okun:
Does it vary a little bit?

28

Steve:
Basically the same place, or if I'll touch elsewhere, it spreads.

Dr. Okun:
Elsewhere on your face, or anywhere on your body?

Steve:
Just on my face.

Dr. Okun:
Where is it usually distributed on your face?

Steve:
Around here, right now it is all over my forehead, my scalp.

Dr. Okun:
Your scalp.

Steve:
This is the highest that it has ever been, so I think it is from scratching here and then go scratching there, and that is how it spreads. I never had it up there before.

Dr. Okun:
Does it itch more or is it more painful?

Steve:
It is kind of, I guess it is itching because it is dry, something like that tingling sensation, not really itching, you want to scratch it.

Dr. Okun:
It is kind of deep?

Steve:
Right, I can't really explain it, especially the one under my chin; the one in my nose, it doesn't really itch. Like I was saying, I had that white, it doesn't look like pus but is like, the harder you press, the stuff just kept coming out, and I never had that before. In boot camp I never had that before. Just the open lesions, but now it is like I had this white stuff collected throughout my nose, and I had one up here, and the harder you press, it doesn't show anything on the surface, like if I just start pressing at random anywhere and this white stuff keeps coming out, and it is just tons coming out, and it is just like a little sac, it doesn't want to come out, but you barely brush it like that, and it pops and a little sac that comes out, it pops. I never had anything like that before.

Dr. Okun:
It is getting worse then ...

Steve:
It is like my nose, if I start pressing probably it will start coming out, like I said you wipe, and it's barely red from being pressed and that is it, and the next day I wake up, and it is a humongous sore, like I have been with a visegrip or something, it's unreal. I never had that before, it is about the only difference. What it is, I don't know

Dr. Okun:
Now you said they did culture it, and it is definitely Herpes I.

Steve:
They never really went into detail, but they said it was Herpes I, they never would tell me whether it was sexually transmitted. He said it was either that, one doctor said, it was

either that or stress, going through boot camp, and it was a new adjustment and the whole nine yards, but hell, I was adjusted in the Marines after two years and I still had outbreaks.

Dr. Okun:
How long were you in the service for?

Steve:
Four years.

Dr. Okun:
I am going to go ahead, and we are going to ask you some questions now. The first question is: Do you feel the same alone as you do with other people?

Steve:
Sometimes.

Dr. Okun:
And would you rather be by yourself or with someone else?

Steve:
Someone else.

Dr. Okun:
Are you ashamed of your thoughts?

Steve:
Sometimes.

Dr. Okun:
Do you feel people should like you?

ERASING SCARS

Steve:
Yes.

Dr. Okun:
What don't you like about yourself?

Steve:
Well, at this moment in my life, I am not too productive, that is. My career, is about the main thing. It lowers my personality, that is, some.

Dr. Okun:
What kind of work do you do?

Steve:
I worked at a refinery and they had a lay off, and I was the second to last one that got hired, so ...

Dr. Okun:
If you could spit in someone's face and tell them a thing or two, what would you tell them?

Steve:
First of all, I wouldn't spit in someone's face; I don't know what I would tell them.

Evangelita:
Can you think of the worst insult that you ever heard? What is the worst thing that anyone called you?

Steve:
Probably dumb jock, I heard that a million times, since I was a kid.

Evangelita:
Oh, so that dates back to the people that raised you?

Steve:
Oh, no, that came from friends and not friends, and people that I knew but I wasn't social with, they really didn't like me, and called me dumb jock, and all this circulated around town, and it came back to me, I was labeled that for many years, football, body building.

Dr. Okun:
Were you a football player?

Steve:
You always hear that.

Dr. Okun:
What position in football did you play?

Steve:
Fullback, punter, and linebacker, nine years of it.

Dr. Okun:
Who are you madly in love with?

Steve:
Well, my girlfriend says myself, but ... (laughter) I concentrate a lot on my physique and stuff, I shouldn't do that as much as I should do other things, but I love my girlfriend a lot. I put a lot of pressure on myself, trying to uphold my physique, and I stress out a lot if I can't make it to the gym, if I have to work late or losing weight or strength, I don't look as good as I did last year, but a lot of it stays in my mind and I take it out on others, it's one of the main problems I have. It stays in my

unconscious a lot. People who see you the way you looked two years ago, it is like you have to uphold that, if you can't, the whole world goes down the tubes, I feel that a lot of this has to do with the hormones, I know that.

Dr. Okun:
Let me ask you, with the condition on your face, has that affected your training and your interaction, let's say, with your girlfriend?

Steve:
Yes, she doesn't touch me when I have an outbreak. I told her not to.

Dr. Okun:
What kind of effect has that had on your relationship?

Steve:
Oh, she thinks I've had sex with a million women, and prostitutes and all of this when I was overseas, and I keep telling her, and I say no, I had this in boot camp. They say it was stress related, simple, everyday common cold sore or fever blister. We had some problems at first, but we have been together four years. It is kind of like she forgets about it.

Dr. Okun:
In this country alone, there are forty million people with Herpes II infection, and one hundred million with Herpes I and II, everybody has been exposed to it. Who has slapped you lately?

Steve:
I haven't had a slap in a while. It happened about two years ago, my girlfriend's friend.

Dr. Okun:
She slapped you?

Steve:
I told her a remark, something I didn't approve of what she had done.

Evangelita:
What is the worst cursing word you ever used?

Steve:
The worst curse word?

Evangelita:
Yes.

Steve:
Probably that day, I threw some good vocabulary terms at her, and that is why I got backhanded. It's the only time I ever got slapped.

Dr. Okun:
Do you want to grow apart from everyone?

Steve:
I like being different. If that is the correct answer.

Evangelita:
Do you think a tree can grow, with many trees around it, just as it would whether there were a tree around it or not? How much does a tree depend on other trees?

Steve:
It shouldn't.

Evangelita:
How would you describe yourself? How much do you depend on others?

Steve:
A lot.

Evangelita:
And do you think you are against yourself for that? Do you think you give too much emphasis on what others think of you?

Steve:
Right.

Evangelita:
As opposed to, do I like myself?

Steve:
That is it.

Evangelita:
For how I have to grow? In other words a tree has a responsibility to be a tree and to get as tall as it can be, in the same way that we do as human beings; we're put on this earth, and we have a responsibility to grow and do as we hear inside of us, something in you tells you what you should do. Do you hear yourself talk to yourself? Do you have a recurrent saying that you tell yourself, something over and over again, what do you tell yourself over and over again, like at nine o'clock this morning what were you telling yourself?

Steve:
I wish I was waking up to get ready to go to a job.

Evangelita:
Were you reading the newspaper?

Steve:
For jobs.

Evangelita:
You were reading the newspaper? Ah, and then what happened? Did you get bitter?

Steve:
It didn't have too much to offer.

Evangelita:
And what did you do, did you put the paper in the garbage?

Steve:
I just folded it.

Evangelita:
Did you sit on it?

Steve:
My parents were reading it, and then they had to get back to work.

Evangelita:
So, has the world ended for you because there is no job out there, as you see it?

Steve:
It feels like it. I have bills, and I don't have any income right now, and it is rough.

ERASING SCARS

Evangelita:
We have a beautiful poem for you tonight.

Dr. Okun:
(Reads) This is called "The Disease Song."

Evangelita:
See if it represents you.

Dr. Okun:
I have to beg on my knees,
and say please, give me what I deserve.
No way, says the manager.
But I barely have food to eat,
said the worker.
GNP is down, tough shit, says the manager
Or the owner.
I need a day to take care of my children,
who are gone, said the poor worker.
Tut, tut, we can't have that here,
workers are not people,
says the Manager.
But I am making so much profit for you,
says the poor worker.
No, you are not, says the Manager.
I have to pay you, I have to. I have to pay you,
I have to pay rent, and you think I am made
out of money, when in fact I am starving, but I
worked to get where I am, and you want to
take all my money and you don't want to work
for it, you don't know all my costs.
It is the bottom line, you cost me plenty,
he said. But I simply asked for what was

38

fair, he said, the worker, a small portion of
malpractice insurance, health insurance, and
insurance, insurance.
I simply want to be paid for my
work. No, said the Owner, you want to steal
my money, and I won't have it. You want more
than we can offer, because I don't have a
penny. Well, how much do your commercials
cost, or your building? Oh, that is not my
money, you have to get up he said,
because you are too slow, you have to increase your
encounter
ratio he said, because you are too slow.

Evangelita:
Any comments?

Steve:
I like that.

Evangelita:
Does it represent us, you?

Steve:
To some degree.

Evangelita:
Do you feel that you have been misjudged, mistreated, and misseen by just about everyone?

Steve:
No, not everyone.

Evangelita:
Has anyone seen you just in the way you are hoping for?

Steve:
No.

Evangelita:
Is that a reason to want to die?

Steve:
I think about it a lot.

Evangelita:
Have you tried to commit suicide?

Steve:
Oh, no. Not that much.

Evangelita:
Have you ever put a gun to your temple?

Steve:
Oh, no.

Evangelita:
Have you wished to?

Steve:
No.

Evangelita:
Have you wished you had the guts to do that? When you read the newspaper and you heard that someone committed suicide, do you think that is right to do, or not right to do?

Steve:
Not right to do. I don't think it's right.

Evangelita:
Has that prevented you from doing it?

Steve:
Yes.

Evangelita:
What has prevented you truly from committing suicide?

Steve:
I think about it a lot sometimes, lately I think about it. I think it would be like a total relief of all problems.

Evangelita:
Have you buried yourself and performed your own funeral?

Steve:
Oh, no. I thought about it.

Evangelita:
Okay. When you were three years old ... do you have orchards? trees?

Steve:
Yes.

Evangelita:
Did you used to wander around the flowers? Did you like to smell them?

Steve:
Yes.

Evangelita:
What is your favorite color of the flower?

Steve:
The petals.

Evangelita:
Petals?

Steve:
Red.

Evangelita:
Red. Do you think that is less red now, because you don't have a job? If you went to the orchards, and could smell the rose again, would you say it would smell not as beautiful because you don't have a job?

Steve:
No. It would smell the same.

Evangelita:
But there is something in you that feels that because of all that you have been through, that somehow that rose does not smell, you cannot go out there and smell the rose anymore, because there is too much pain in your life, and you can't handle it, and you feel you can't go out there and smell the rose no more, and you are going to shut the door and bar people out. And I have a poem written by a woman in the nineteenth century, and her name is Christina Rossetti:

Who Shall Deliver Me?
God strengthen me to bear myself,
That heaviest weight of all to bear

Inalienable weight of care.

All others are outside myself
I lock my door and bar them out.
The turmoil, tedium, gad-about.

I lock my door upon myself
And bar them out; but who shall wall,
Self from myself, most loathed of all?

If I could once lay down myself
And start self-purged upon the race
That all must run! Death runs apace.

If I could set aside myself,
And start with lightened heart upon
The road by all men overgone!

God harden me against myself,
This coward with pathetic voice
Who craves for ease and rest and joys:

Myself arch-traitor to myself;
My hollowest friend, my deadliest foe,
My clog whatever road I go.

Yet One there is can curb myself
Can roll the strangling load from me,
break off the yoke and set me free.

Evangelita:
Who is her enemy?

ERASING SCARS

Steve:
Myself.

Evangelita:
What do you think you have most against yourself?

Steve:
Image.

Evangelita:
Image. Did you like the way the sky looked today?

Steve:
No.

Evangelita:
What did you like today?

Steve:
Nothing special.

Evangelita:
Do you prefer a rainy day to a sunny day?

Steve:
It doesn't really matter.

Evangelita:
But you used to like rainy days? Did you ever ice skate?

Steve:
[Nods.]

Evangelita:
Did you roller-skate?

44

Steve:
Yes.

Evangelita:
When did you roller-skate?

Steve:
When? Many years ago.

Evangelita:
And you were good? Is that your favorite thing to do?

Steve:
Not my favorite, but I used to do it a lot, I could really skate.

Evangelita:
What did you feel when you roller-skated? Did you remember that you don't have a job?

Steve:
That I was young again.

Evangelita:
Young again, okay. Is the rose young again? Is anything not young again? What is not young other than your dirty thoughts? Which is the worst thought you ever had today? What was your worst miserable thought that you had today? "God strengthen me to bear myself," like she says. Do you ask God to help you bear yourself? Can you stand yourself anymore?

Steve:
Sometimes I do ask.

Evangelita:
Do you feel you are too much for you? And God has given you this weight to deal with, and you just cannot handle you, you cannot handle you. Do you get up in the morning praying, how am I going to do with me? Are you a big burden to yourself? That is what she is saying, and she is a woman, she is saying, I am too much of a burden to myself. I can't deal with me, I don't know what I want, because when I do get it, I don't want it. Are you that kind? You get what you want and then you don't want it, you get a slap in the face, and then you say I don't want it but meantime you look for it, you know. This is the song of all of us, you represent every one of us, we are just like you are. What we are trying to do is to put opposites together in our lives. Do you think you are more angry than grateful? Do you think you have about a thousand things you should be grateful for that you are not, because you don't want to remember gratitude? Is there something in you that wants to spit at God? Do you think if you got the herpes on the face, who gave it to you? Who invented it? A. McDonalds? B. Burger King? C. Don's Sea Food? Who created the Herpes? The next-door neighbor? Who created it? Who did it? Who did it?

Steve:
I guess myself.

Evangelita:
Who?

Steve:
I guess myself.

Evangelita:
You created the virus?

Steve:
It comes from somewhere.

Evangelita:
But you did not create it, who created the virus?

Steve:
The Lord did.

Evangelita:
Do you think so? Do you think there is something in us that is like the virus itself? Do you think we trick ourselves? Dr. Okun just described the virus. What does it do? It sleeps ten days, and when it feels like it, it comes out, and then it goes right back in, right into the nerve cells; now why does it not stay asleep, why does it come out? What brings it out, do you think? We have studied ten years, the virus. We have understood, finally, what it is in us that brings it out, and also how people are like the virus. Did you ever meet somebody that tells you something and then changes their mind and disappoints you? And they keep you all in expectation and all of a sudden there is nothing, disappointment. And when they offer it to you, they are pumping you up and getting you all excited for something, and then the next week is like a hang-up, a hang-up call, there is nothing, like you meet somebody that shakes your hand and kicks your ass. I mean, I am sorry to use that bad language.

Steve:
It is alright.

Evangelita:
You know, but that is the way it is.

Steve:
Uh huh.

Evangelita:
That is the way the herpes fools the cell. The poor cell, the good healthy cell, thinks there is a friend coming, because it acts just like a friend; then it injects itself, and then it makes that cell totally possessed, and then it does what it wants to do with it.

Dr. Okun:
When you look at the cell microscopically, you see that on the membrane, the cell membrane, it actually has little spikes, and it comes in and it attaches itself to your skin cell membranes by these spikes. The fooling mechanism is that it makes your skin cell feel that it is reproducing its own genetic material or DNA in order to take over the cell, it's a fooling mechanism.

Evangelita:
That's what it does; do you think there is anything in us that wants to fool God? We tell God, no, that beautiful carnation is not red anymore, because I don't have a job today And I am not going to smell your beautiful flowers, dear God, no way, because I got insulted today. I am being here buried alive. Have you felt you have been buried alive?

Steve:
Yes.

Evangelita:
And you are alive, and in the meantime, you are being buried. Okay, we are going to tell you; Eli Siegel, the founder of Aesthetic Realism in 1940, described that in all human beings,

that is exactly like the herpes virus, and it is called 2-A Pleasure and all of us have it, and it is why everyone on this earth has the herpes virus and it doesn't come out, we all have it, we all can have it, all of us, because of that tendency in us to make less of God's Work. To make that beautiful flower less red because we want to blame God for everything, so we take the color out of reality, and it is called 2-A Pleasure, and you can read along with it if you like. And any questions, if you want to stop, you can ask us, and we will stop.

Steve:
[Reads from *Self and World,* "2-A Pleasure Described" by Eli Siegel]

> "It is to be presumed that every self has two sides. What one side likes, the other side doesn't."

Evangelita:
Do you think that is true?

Steve:
"The 'bad' side has been talked about a great deal but has not been permitted heretofore to talk adequately in its own behalf."

Evangelita:
Do you think what one side of you likes, the other side doesn't? Like sometimes, you feel that you want to have breakfast, but something in you says, No, don't eat anymore, you are getting fat.

Steve:
No, I eat, I love food.

Evangelita:
Ah, do you love food?

Steve:
I follow a good diet. I love to eat.

Evangelita:
Sometimes you don't eat? Every day you get up full of appetite, you want to eat, every day? You have never gotten up not feeling hungry?

Steve:
If I am depressed or whatever.

Evangelita:
Okay.

Steve:
I eat, but I think about being depressed after I am done eating.

Evangelita:
So, one side of you liked the egg a week ago, but another side of you didn't like it Tuesday, because something happened to you. And that is what we are trying to explain. Why do we have to not like what we have always liked, because something bad happened to us. Why do we take it out on the egg, why do we take it out on the flower, why is that? We are going to understand that through what Mr. Siegel wrote.

Steve:
(Reads)

"Here is it permitted to talk in the first person and show how 'wonderful' it is. To be sure, there is also the rebuttal by the whole self.

The Self:

Like every other human being, I am in a fight between two kinds of pleasure. In order to decide between the two, I must see both for what they are. I have in the past accented the pains (very great) which have come with my having the pleasure which Aesthetic Realism calls 'ego' or 2-A pleasure. If this pleasure is greater than the other, it would be unwise to give it up. It would be sanity, good sense to continue it. Let me try to make this pleasure as attractive as possible.

2-A Self:

1. It seems to give me a feeling of pure individuality where I don't have to undergo the 'humdrum' competition with other persons that seems to make up such a great part of the present world.

2. I can endlessly despise, and the more I despise the more, apparently logically, my own ego is glorified.

3. I get a sense of triumph from being 'invisible' from humans."

Evangelita:

That's like the virus.

Steve:
(Reads)
> "I can hide with great unconscious glee."

Evangelita:
And I can come out in ten days when I want to.

Steve:
(Reads)
> "4. I am in touch with perfection; the boring and imperfect have been nullified.
>
> 5. I can make fun of everything I want.
>
> 6. Matter, objects no longer seem obstructions. I have done away with pavements, walls, furniture, stone. I am in nothing, and free.
>
> 7. I can make expeditions into the other world, which I still see as shadows, and at my leisure pretend I am part of it. This gives an added fillip to my triumph.
>
> 8. I can talk of my pains eloquently, and fool people as to their cause and meaning.
>
> 9. I can be a deceptive emperor; be present and not present in a room; know the time and not know the time; exist and not exist; and have myself, myself, myself while I fool everything and am not affected by anything."

Evangelita:
That is a description of the virus itself.

Steve:
(Reads)

"(I can pretend I am affected.)

> 10. I (sometimes called Ego) know this
> pleasure. It is what I want, and I'll use pain,
> pain, pain from the world to get it; pretend I
> haven't got it; and justify my continuing to
> have it under opposition.

> **The Whole Self:**
> I should know this (the above); I know it. But
> I, the whole self, want the other pleasure. It is
> greater, it is honest, and it has more than this.
> And I don't have to use pain to get it. It does
> not make guilt. It is the really indescribable
> pleasure from seeing things wholly, honestly,
> wonderfully, humorously, excitingly, truly as
> they are. This pleasure would take the rest of
> time to describe. It is infinite. It is 1-A
> pleasure, Real Pleasure.

Evangelita:
What do you think Mr. Siegel is talking about?

Steve:
What makes it come out.

Evangelita:
Do you think that every time we make less of God's world
something bad happens to us? Why do you think God made
oranges, when was the last time you liked the shape of the
orange?

ERASING SCARS

Steve:
The last time I liked the shape ...

Evangelita:
The shape of the orange.

Steve:
I never thought about it.

Evangelita:
Or the shape of the ... What is your favorite flower?

Steve:
Carnation.

Evangelita:
Carnations, are you like that, are you like the carnation?

Steve:
I have shape and color.

Evangelita:
Do you have color? Do you have shape? Do you have weight? (Pointing to a bowl of fruit) That has weight. Is your hair different from your toes? Is the petal different from the stem? Are your ears different from your nails? We are made exactly the same way as every object. Look at the banana. Does it have an inside? Do you? Do you like it in there?

Steve:
No. I'd trade for the banana.

Evangelita:
You'd rather be a banana.

Steve:
In fact I have one in my truck; I eat them anywhere.

Evangelita:
You like bananas, what is your favorite fruit?

Steve:
Pineapples and bananas.

Evangelita:
If you touch the banana, and you thank God for making the banana, touch it and feel it, and is that from God a gift, because no one can make bananas, I am sorry, I don't care how much money you have, but you can't make a banana, you can make a lot of money, yes, but you can have an infinite amount of money but if you are hungry and only you had the banana, and you haven't eaten in three days, maybe four, maybe a week, do you think this millionaire would give up his money to have food? Who wouldn't give up everything to have food? After five days of not eating or maybe knowing that it might be ten?

Steve:
You have to be insane.

Evangelita:
Okay, do you think that is insanity, insanity is what the poem is about. Why do we put our values not on, what really means something to us, if we don't have the banana or we don't have food, that comes from God, we are not going to make it. Money is going to buy what God has made already. But I never heard God put a price on the banana. I mean, when he made the banana, he didn't say, "Now you Peter, you got to sell my

banana at fifty cents each, and then next year, a dollar, do you understand?" You see, man thinks he has a right to take God's fish and put a price on it, and I am going to starve you, you know, because if you don't make what I want, you are dead. And this is how it is, and we have to take that; why do we have to take that? Because we didn't express ourselves, there is something in us, like the virus itself, we "hide with unconscious glee." We can put prices on things that we know people can't afford, that is contempt. It is what runs the world right now, but everybody would give up everything to have a banana, if they haven't eaten in five days, even sex. If you have a man, and you know you have been trained, you know in the Army and the Marines or whatever, and you know that if you have been out two weeks without food, and there are ballerinas at a bar dancing, enticing you to come to them, and there is a lot of food there, where do you think the men are going to go to, eat? or have sex with the naked girls?

Steve:
Probably have sex.

Evangelita:
After ten days of not eating? Do you really think they are really going to go to the naked girls?

Steve:
I would have something and then go for the sex.

Evangelita:
But first what are they going to do?

Steve:
I would go for the food first.

Evangelita:
They are all going to go for the food, believe me, when it comes to food. Okay, two people are sitting on a sofa, and they are making love, passionate love, and a fire breaks out; what is going to win?

Steve:
They're going to run.

Dr. Okun:
Survival.

Evangelita:
Okay, now you know. Not just survival, but it is an instinct in us, so that is the way it is, so if you don't want to go back and appreciate and respect God's word, God's world, you are not being true to yourself because you come from it, and you don't have a price tag on you. Do you understand? Your Mommie could not have paid enough to have you, you know, did she pray for you? Did she want a chubby little kid like you?

Steve:
I guess.

Evangelita:
Were you her first?

Steve:
Second, I have an older sister.

Evangelita:
You have a sister, but you are her little boy?

Steve:
That's it.

Evangelita:
Your mother could not, no matter how much money she had, if she wanted little Steve to come, no money was going to make you. That is why, when money is not there, is not the time to hate God. But unfortunately, that is what we do, and that is when we welcome disease. That is when we welcome disease, because we are not being true to ourselves. We are having our way, which is the ego way. We damn God, and not appreciate, what is there to be appreciated.

Dr. Okun:
The effect of this is to lower the immunity system, and you allow the viruses to come out, and so what we are talking about, is how do you use the fact that you have been laid off, how do you use the fact of the mounting bills, how do you use the way you have been seen, and do you feel like a Kleenex, that someone used, and then threw out, when it was convenient for them?

Steve:
Right.

Evangelita:
That is what we do with God and he has to take it; when we don't want to see the yellow color in the banana, we don't want to, why should we? Now, this is what we are trying to understand: there are two sides to the self, the side that wants to have contempt, and the side that wants to have respect, and you don't have to get rid of either one. You can have good contempt for someone that wants to make money off of you

and not pay you, someone that wants to demean you and make less of you, they are foolish, because they are going to feel guilty about making less of God's world, that is where guilt comes from. Guilt comes from us not giving value to what things have. We feel ashamed. When you blush ... why do you think people blush?

Steve:
They are ashamed.

Evangelita:
And why does it show emotionally?

Steve:
Guilt.

Evangelita:
Isn't that interesting? So it is not something you can control. You are just made that way. If you are caught telling a lie, you will blush, you know. And that is not learned anywhere, that is something you are born with, if you are telling a lie, you are going to blush. And what have you been lying to yourself about for the past ten years, who tried to trip you up?

Steve:
I can't blame anybody else. The reason I am here is because of myself.

Evangelita:
Did anybody try to trip you up? Who is Mike? Do you know anybody called Michael?

Steve:
My middle name.

Evangelita:
Middle name of who?

Steve:
Me.

Evangelita:
That is you? Okay, do you think you know you?

Steve:
I guess not thoroughly.

Evangelita:
Do you want to? Because it is what the problem is God has given you; but he hasn't given you, I guess, time to understand you; do you have time to understand you?

Steve:
I guess I am scared to really know.

Evangelita:
Do you think you ran out of time? Do you have time to know yourself? Do you think it is possible? Do you think understanding can erase a lot of pain that you have? If you want to know yourself, would you be in as much pain? Do you think you want to rush through you? You don't give yourself a chance. You are too harsh with yourself. What was the worst name you called yourself today, schmuck? What do you call yourself?

Steve:
I don't really know, I can't think of anything.

Evangelita:
Did you ever call yourself dumb?

Steve:
Yeah.

Evangelita:
All the time? Do you have a recurrent dream that keeps happening? The type of dream that keeps recurring all the time?

Steve:
I had something a while back, I can't remember what it was.

Evangelita:
Do you drive a motorcycle? Were you driving any car? Were you climbing anything? Were you sleeping?

Steve:
I don't remember. It was about myself and about my girlfriend, by the time I was done with the dream I was beating her.

Evangelita:
Beating her?

Steve:
A lot of times during my dream I am, like, beating her.

Evangelita:
You are beating her?

Steve:
That is right. She is, like, cheating on me, I know she isn't, but I dream that all the time, every dream I've had, I am beating her.

Evangelita:
Okay, do you think you deserve to be loved? Well, do you think you deserve being loved or slapped? Which do you want her to do, slap you or love you?

Steve:
Love me.

Evangelita:
Do you love yourself? You want her to love you, but then you don't accept yourself. You don't have time to know yourself. You actually are denying her the right to care for you, because you are not ready to care for you yet. You don't approve of yourself. What do you have to do to approve of yourself? What do you have to prove to yourself?

Steve:
I guess it all boils down to hobby, I guess.

Evangelita:
Hobby?

Steve:
The way I look, physique, working out. That is what makes me go from day to day, my image, that is the way I look at it, if I don't have that, everything goes down the drain.

Evangelita:
What are you inside? Inside, do you have an image? Which is better, the image outside of you or the image inside of you?

Steve:
It should be inside.

Evangelita:
Okay.

Steve:
If you don't have that ...

Evangelita:
Okay, because you want to run away from you, see, and God says, "No way." Do you have time to know yourself? What are you, anyway? What is your earliest memory?

Steve:
I can't recall.

Evangelita:
Did you ever have a red ball?

Steve:
Green.

Evangelita:
And what did you do with the ball?

Steve:
I held it in a picture, when I was two years old.

Evangelita:
Do you still have it? When you look at it, what do you want to do, puke?

Steve:
(Nods yes)

Evangelita:
Do you want to laugh?

Steve:
Yeah.

Evangelita:
Can you enjoy your memories?

Steve:
Most of them, I wish I could start over and do it right.

Evangelita:
You can do it, why not? It is never too late.

Steve:
It feels like it.

Evangelita:
Why?

Steve:
I am getting older, I guess.

Evangelita:
Old about what, your ideas, I hope. Who gave you the green ball?

Steve:
My Mom, and I have a picture of it.

Evangelita:
How could you have it all this time? Why didn't you throw it away?

Steve:
I don't have it.

Evangelita:
Who has it?

Steve:
My Mom, I haven't seen it in years.

Evangelita:
And what is your favorite breakfast?

Steve:
Hash browns, and about a dozen-egg omelet.

Evangelita:
Who cooks it for you?

Steve:
I cook it myself.

Evangelita:
Do you want anyone to do anything for you?

Steve:
Yes.

Evangelita:

Who has cooked breakfast for you lately?

Steve:

I make that myself. My parents cook me dinner.

Evangelita:

Do you have a hard time accepting love and encouragement? Are you hard to get along with now, because you don't have a job?

Steve:

I was hard to get along with before I lost my job, not having a job is escalating it. These feelings I already had.

Evangelita:

If you had a wish to ask God, what would it be?

Steve:

To improve my inner self, and hopefully get some income, too. That's the most important thing right now.

Evangelita:

If he grants you that wish, what are you going to give him? What would you like to give your Maker?

Steve:
Church time.

Evangelita:

We have a beautiful psalm that might represent you, Psalm 139. You might know it. See if it represents you. Psalm 139.

Dr. Okun:
Can you read that out loud?

Steve:
A lot of this is written in that weird—you know what I am talking about. It is kind of hard to read out. That is the most I've read in years. All I read is body-building stuff. It really shows.

Evangelita:
No, it does not.

Steve:
(Reads Psalm 139)

Psalm 139

To the chief Musician. A Psalm of David

O Lord, thou hast searched me, and known me. Thou knowest my downsitting and mine uprising, thou understandest my thought afar off.

Thou compassest my path and my lying down, and art acquainted with all my ways.

For there is not a word in my tongue, but lo, O Lord, thou knowest it altogether.

Thou has beset me behind and before, and laid thine hand upon me.

Such knowledge is too wonderful for me; it is high, I cannot attain unto it.

ERASING SCARS

Whither shall I go from thy Spirit? Or whither shall I flee from thy presence?

If I ascend up into heaven, thou art there. If I make my bed in hell, behold, thou art there.

If I take the wings of the morning, and dwell in the uttermost parts of the sea;

Even there shall thy hand lead me, and thy right hand shall hold me.

If I say, "Surely the darkness shall cover me," even the night shall be light about me.

Yea, the darkness hideth not from thee, but the night shineth as the day: the darkness and the light are both alike to thee.

For thou hast possessed my reins; thou hast covered me in my mother's womb.

I will praise thee; for I am fearfully and wonderfully made: marvelous are thy works; and that my soul knoweth right well.

My substance was not hid from thee, when I was made in secret, and curiously wrought in the lowest parts of the earth.

Thine eyes did see my substance, yet being unperfect; and in thy book all my members were written, which in continuance were fashioned, when as yet there was none of them.

How precious also are thy thoughts unto me, O God! How great is the sum of them!

If I should count them, they are more in number than the sand: when I awake, I am still with thee. Surely thou wilt slay the wicked, O God depart from me therefore, ye bloody men.

For they speak against thee wickedly, and thine enemies take thy name in vain.

Do not I hate them, O Lord, that hate thee, and am not I grieved with those that rise up against thee?

I hate them with perfect hatred: I count them mine enemies.

Search me, O God, and know my heart: try me, and know my thoughts:

And see if there be any wicked way in me, and lead me in the way everlasting.

Evangelita:
Do you think God knows where you have been wicked, and where you are very good? And you can't hide from him? Like the herpes virus does, hides. That is the opposite of the herpes virus, because God is light and yet he made you in secret, but for the purpose of giving you life. The herpes virus hides in secret for the purpose of killing you, and in the research that Dr. Okun has seen, it can kill you.

Dr. Okun:
The problem is that it can travel to your brain, and you said it had infected your eye. Did you ever have an ulcer on the eye?

People don't know that about twenty percent of this can go to your brain and give you what is called Herpes Encephalitis, which is an infection of the brain.

Steve:
What type of side effects would that have?

Dr. Okun:
People get comatose, confused, they get headaches. Encephalitis is very severe. It is life-threatening, it is a possible complication. Have you had people that you get very angry at, but you don't express it and it kind of boils inside?

Evangelita:
Okay, that's being hidden, that is not like God, everything he has made you see it, and then when you don't see, you feel it, you are inside of yourself and outside of yourself; but the reason for you to be hidden should be the same reason for you to be open. You see, that is what God does, but he wants you to know yourself, and you can do it if you have time. Would you take time to know yourself? Dear, we all have to do it.

Dr. Okun:
Who is the one person who makes the most out of you, in your life?

Steve:
Probably my mom.

Dr. Okun:
And who would you say makes you into nothing?

Steve:
Who would make me into nothing? I can't think of anyone.

Evangelita:
Who is the person who called you dumb?

Steve:
That's just kids. Childhood.

Evangelita:
Do you think, whenever your opinion of someone that is not smart, like who would that be? Who do you know that you know is not smart?

Dr. Okun:
The stupidest person you know?

Steve:
I know a couple.

Evangelita:
Do you know a lot of them? Do you know more intelligent people or more stupid people? Are you surrounded by a bunch of ...

Steve:
More intelligent.

Evangelita:
More intelligent people. Your attitude is usually to see the keenness in people, their intelligence. Or do you think you go right to where they are not so intelligent, where they are not so smart? There is something in all of us, the first thing we look at, where is the person stupid? Or where does this person not look as good as I do? Do you have that in you?

Steve:
No.

Evangelita:
When you look at other people do you see where they are more beautiful than you or more ugly?

Steve:
Where they look better. See if they look better.

Evangelita:
Okay, do you think this comes from the good side of you or the bad side?

Steve:
The bad side.

Evangelita:
That wants to prove what? What do you want to prove?

Steve:
That I am better.

Evangelita:
Okay. Is that describing the contempt side which creates the herpes? Which is the virus itself, and then the shame that you have shows in your face, believe it or not, you are not blushing, but the thing that you have in your head doesn't change; but I tell you something, if you are proud of how you see God's world, that will not come. It will go away. Because it is a beautiful thing that has happened to you. You are punishing yourself for not being fair to God. You are ashamed of it, and that shows in your face, which I think is very ethical, because in some people it doesn't show on their face, it shows in

another way But all disease comes from not being proud of ourselves for some reason. We either make too much of ourselves and too little of the world, we are not accurate. The only way to be accurate is to study art. The artist looks at the apple or the banana. He is not too good to look at a banana and put it in a painting. He doesn't just gobble it up and that is it. We do, we just gobble up reality we don't want to think about it. But if you give thought to objects like the artist does, then you are going to be respecting your Maker, which is what art does, this is why art is very important. You say you haven't read; what is your favorite book? One of your favorite books?

Steve:
Body Building books, I am fascinated with World War II aircraft, I know a good bit about that.

Evangelita:
So do you like history? Well, do you have a history?

Steve:
I have to learn that first.

Evangelita:
In other words, use World War II to know yourself, what mistakes did they make? Do you know?

Steve:
I wouldn't say they made the mistakes, they told them to go so they had to.

Evangelita:
Do you think we are too good to look at our mistakes? Okay, so we have committed a great error, thinking less of God's world, thinking we should be better than it, in any way or any form;

but then you are not too good to look at it, that is why that psalm is so beautiful: God knows my thoughts, I don't; do you know your thoughts, all of them? You don't, do you? God does, he knows everything about you, he made you, you are just a little baby just born, in terms of what you know about yourself; but we don't have the time, we say; why not, why don't you have the time to know yourself? What else is more important?

Steve:
Nothing really, just learning from it, I guess.

Evangelita:
So you are ashamed of it, and it shows on your face? It is a beautiful thing if you know what I mean, because you are not proud of it. But I think if you do every day, write one thing you like, even if it is just an apple—you don't know how long it took God to make an apple, do you know?

Steve:
No.

Evangelita:
But if you took the time to be grateful to everything that is not ourselves, which nothing is, the chair that you're are sitting on, you didn't make it, did you?

Steve:
No.

Evangelita:
Did you make the clothes you wear? Did you make your shoes? Did you make your hair? What did you make? Terror for yourself?

Steve:
I sure did, that is what I did. That is about it.

Dr. Okun:
You see, what it is, is the disintegration you have when a disease process is coming on; we think that we have to have this fight going on, you feel angry, you have been thrown out of a job, and you have this anger with that, and there are things that you should be grateful for; and all of us feel that we have to have these two things fighting all the time. You could be angry about being unfairly thrown out of a job, but it doesn't mean that you have to forget everything that you should be grateful for and it is this disintegration, this banging and fighting within ourselves, that causes the disease process. Mr. Siegel said the definition of disease is "lack of ease" Do you feel nervous a lot of times? Jumpy? Not like a calm Mediterranean blue water, more like a stormy ocean?

Steve:
Yeah.

Evangelita:
This is what aesthetics does, you can read from "The Aesthetic Method in Self-Conflict" about aesthetics. Aesthetics is beautiful, which is what you want to be, you want to be beautiful, right? To like your image?

> (Reads) **Self and World,** pp. 96-98—"The Aesthetic Method in Self-Conflict" by Eli Siegel
>
> Aesthetics makes the essential superiority and inferiority feelings in man a working team, a

team of oneness. We can't kick out either Jamison's arrogance or his shyness. They are both part of him. They are to be made one, and they can be. Right now, they are in conflict; that is, submissiveness and domineeringness are close in Jamison's mind, and yet they are separate. Mr. Jamison wants them to be close; he also wants them go away from each other. Togetherness is fighting separation in his mind. He is having a bad time.

Aesthetics here should be seen as a possible job of engineering. It is clear that Jamison has to feel yielding and managing at once. Otherwise, he will shuttle unhealthily. The question Jamison and other people face is: Can, in one mind, feelings represented by superiority exist with feelings represented by inferiority? Can we be both humble and bold at 3:30 P.M., Tuesday?—Only art shows that the answer is, Yes. If metaphysics, logic, ethics, psychology, can say yes, too—it's because they are, this while, what art is.

Take Whitman's *Song of Myself*. Whitman yields himself to what he sees; to earth, to people; and he is proud doing so. Art shows we can be proud in seeing clearly, without rigmarole, or pretense, that we are less than we can be. Art makes for pride in the fact, even when that fact is against ego in the narrow sense, or 2-A. (Self having false importance by being opposed to the world is termed by us 2-A.) In Whitman's *Song of Myself* a man becomes exultant through modesty, modest through exultation. The intense, wide, great fact sweeps Whitman truly; he yields and he has a feeling of deep independence and pride. Where even a Whitman does not feel this, it's because art is not complete. As far as Whitman is an artist— and this is very far; and as far as he gives himself, without interior vanity wriggling, to what is, he feels that *he* is, and he is proud. Jamison should know this.

If a person feels inferior, the first question to ask is, What does he feel inferior about? I don't believe that psychiatrists have asked this question rightly. If a person is unable to do something, or if he doesn't know something, and he knows this neatly, definitely, he will not feel inferior in the morbid sense. He would feel at least he knew himself; and would be proud of that. In other words, in yielding to the facts about himself courageously, truly, there would be a self-approval. Further, if what he desired were good, and he really desired it, he would also approve of himself. Every true desire has action going with it. In following, honestly, steadily, without trickery, a true desire, we feel proud. All this means: yielding to the facts can make us proud.

In aesthetics, there is more true yielding to the facts than elsewhere. Suppose a writer were confessing in his manuscript something which was actually so, and offhand seemed depreciating of him. Having the courage to say what was true of himself, for the purpose of saying it truly and having it known as it was— would he not feel proud? The real critical feeling is always proud: whether of oneself or of others. The real critical feeling, however, seldom occurs.

If knowing oneself were to make inevitably for inferiority, certainly many people should be told not to know themselves. But even the most gentle psychotherapists would hesitate to say people should not know themselves. Behind this hesitation is the feeling that when people know themselves, they truly can approve of themselves because they know what they are. *No self can truly know itself and be ashamed.*

Well, this is what Mr. Siegel is teaching us, I want to be beautiful too, why not, and I want to be beautiful inside and outside.

Dr. Okun:
Page 96 of *Self and World* by Mr. Siegel, "Aesthetics makes the essential superiority and inferiority feelings in man a working team, a team of oneness. We can't kick out either Jamison's arrogance or his shyness."

Evangelita:
Do you think this has to do with the dream you had?

Steve:
Somewhat.

Evangelita:
It is like, if you feel you are submissive, but then you want to show that you have power, too. Do you feel you have been taken over by this girl, therefore, she is fooling you in some way? You say you are jealous or whatever, but she is not doing anything like that, so you go from being very ... would you read that again?

Dr. Okun:
"We can't kick out either Jamison's arrogance or his shyness."

Evangelita:
How would you describe yourself right now, shy or arrogant?

Steve:
Shy.

Evangelita:
Shy, right, but in the dream beating the girlfriend up, were you arrogant?

Steve:
(Nods yes)

Evangelita:
So you can't kick out that side of you, and you can't kick out the other side of you, and you shouldn't, because you are both. Why should you be less than you are? Why can't you have

shyness, arrogance, and all of it? If you are shy to be fooling people, then you are like the virus. It is going to come out on your face. If you are shy because you honestly don't know, and you shouldn't be arrogant because you don't know, you don't know, my name, you don't know where I am from, that kind of thing that is fine, but the purpose is to show who you are, not fool, like the virus does. It goes in there and it fools you, so it is the purpose that is going to have to change; you don't have to get rid of any quality you have, none. Only the purpose, because the purpose of your arrogance or the purpose of your shyness should all be to love God's world and to make anyone stronger not to show that you are more important.

Dr. Okun:
(Reads)

> "We can't kick out either Jamison's arrogance or his shyness. They are both part of him. They are to be made one, and they can be. Right now, they are in conflict; that is, submissiveness and domineeringness are close in Jamison's mind, and yet they are separate. Mr. Jamison wants them to be close; he also wants them to go away from each other. Togetherness is fighting separation in his mind. He is having a bad time. Aesthetics here should be seen as a possible job of engineering. It is clear that Jamison has to feel yielding and managing at once. Otherwise, he will shuttle unhealthily. The question Jamison and other people face is: Can, in one mind, feelings represented by superiority exist with

> feelings represented by inferiority? Can we be
> both humble and bold at 3:30P.M., Tuesday?"

Evangelita:
Humble and bold. When we read that Psalm, was it humble
and bold? That psalm or the first poem that you read, "God
strengthen me to bear myself? It has boldness, but it has
humility. God strengthen me to bear myself. Bold, but it has
tremendous humility? You can have both. You can be humble
but bold. You don't have to give up anything you have.

Dr. Okun:
(Reads)

> "Only art shows that the answer is, Yes. If
> metaphysics, logic, ethics, psychology, can say
> yes, too—it's because they are, this while, what
> art is. Take Whitman's *Song of Myself*.
> Whitman yields himself to what he sees; to
> earth, to people; and he is proud doing so."

Evangelita:
Like when you look at the carnation, look at the red carnation:
are you yielding to it?

Steve:
Yes

Evangelita:
You are attracted to it?

Steve:
Right

ERASING SCARS

Evangelita:
You can't say its ugly?

Steve:
No.

Evangelita:
You know the colors attract you, it is not something that you created, right? Where is it from, you being attracted to the carnation? What would you call that in you that is attracted by that carnation? The colors, shape.

Steve:
The color.

Evangelita:
Right now, you have the artist's mind, that is what the artist does, he honors what you have. See, you have honored the carnation, but the artist goes a little step further, he paints it or he writes a poem about it and he thinks about it. He becomes one with his Maker; you have to take one more step, let's say, today. I am not too good to honor the carnation, I am not too good to honor the banana because something in you is so arrogant all the time, I don't have to honor anything. When you are an artist you are humble, which is the same as your boldness, and it is eternal, that is eternal, that carnation. I don't care what you think about it, but she's going to be here, and you're not, I mean flowers, no matters how many bombs in World War II would destroy flowers, everywhere they threw them, they still grew didn't they, and they still grow after Vietnam, don't they? And no matter what you think, whether you see them or not, they are going to grow and they will wait for you, dear friend, to like them. God waits for us to honor his

world, and that is why he has made a carnation. He didn't make General Motors, did he? Or AT&T? But that may not be here, but God's carnation, believe it or not, they will be, like the virus and that is why we can't be fooled by that bad side in us that wants to think, my way is my way, and then you get the little pimples on your face. It all comes from that. Mr. Siegel says, "No self can truly know itself and be ashamed."

Do you believe that is true about you? If you know yourself more, would you be less ashamed of yourself or more ashamed?

Steve:
Less ashamed.

Evangelita:
Okay, that is what we are trying to do.

Dr. Okun:
(Reads)

> "Take Whitman's *Song of Myself.* Whitman yields himself to what he sees; to earth, to people; and he is proud doing so. Art shows we can be proud in seeing clearly, without rigmarole, or pretense, that we are less than we can be."

Evangelita:
Do you care to comment?

Steve:
It describes myself.

Evangelita:
How? (No response)

Evangelita:
Do you ever make your bed?

Steve:
Most of the time.

Evangelita:
Most of the time, but not all the time? Why not?

Steve:
I am lazy.

Evangelita:
But do you think that has to do with aesthetics? Do you ever go out of your house without combing your hair?

Steve:
No.

Evangelita:
Why not?

Steve:
Because it is me.

Evangelita:
Okay, you got it, so if it is you, you are going to take care of you; but the world is you, too. Because what do you have in your mind that is not the world? Where does the world start?

Steve:
Where does it start?

Evangelita:
Yes.

Steve:
It starts with yourself.

Evangelita:
With your fingertips, everything that is not you. Can you name something that is not world right here, the floor that you are touching, the chair that you are sitting in? The only thing that I know about you is what I have in me, what God has given me, and everything else is not me, everything, and it seems that there are more things that are not us than are us, so we need to think about them; we have a big job. Do you have time? Do you? Make time. What does time mean to you?

Steve:
Something that I need to utilize more efficiently.

Evangelita:
What makes you sad?

Steve:
It could be anything.

Evangelita:
Do you cry easily?

Steve:
I have before.

Evangelita:
You have? When was the last time that you cried?

Steve:
About two months ago.

Evangelita:
What happened?

Steve:
Depressed.

Evangelita:
Do you have a pet?

Steve:
A dog.

Evangelita:
What is his name?

Steve:
Potpourri.

Evangelita:
Does he love you? Does he make you happy?

Steve:
Oh yeah.

Evangelita:
So when you cry, you cry with him?

Steve:
Oh, no.

Evangelita:
You are ashamed?

Steve:
He stinks too much to get on my bed.

Evangelita:
You are ashamed to cry even in front of your dog? When you cry, do you close the door?

Steve:
(Nods no)

Evangelita:
Do you think you are too much of a man to have anybody see your tears?

Steve:
(Nods yes)

Evangelita:
So you will not show your tears to anybody?

Steve:
I try not to.

Evangelita:
Because you are very, very tough. Meantime, the other side comes out, and then what do you do? God made you tearful, you know, we all have a tear in our eye? How long have you had him? Potpourri?

Steve:
Four years.

Evangelita:
Are you afraid to get married?

Steve:
(Nods yes)

Evangelita:
How afraid are you? Terrified?

Steve:
Terrified.

Evangelita:
If God asks you, would you rather have the herpes on your face than get married, what would you rather have?

Steve:
Stop the herpes.

Evangelita:
So you'd rather get married?

Steve:
No.

Evangelita:
You'd rather have the herpes than get married?

Steve:
I'd rather have that go away.

Evangelita:
Are you very frightened of marriage?

Steve:
A little bit.

Evangelita:
Is she pressuring you to marry?

Steve:
She talks about it more than I do.

Evangelita:
Is that why you are not working?

Steve:
Oh, no.

Evangelita:
Do you know what works in you?

Steve:
No.

Evangelita:
Do you like to disappoint people?

Steve:
I try not to.

Evangelita:
Are you using this job not to get married? If you don't work, how bad of a partner are you? Do you do this to keep the thought of marriage away as far away as you can? Would you like to hug marriage or kick it?

Steve:
I don't want to think about it, too much. Not at the moment, that is.

Evangelita:
But do you think somewhere you do want to get married? And somewhere you don't, so what one side of you likes the other side doesn't? And that is your conflict? And you are ashamed and you got the blisters on your face. Do you want to be happy? or do you want to be sad? When do you feel strong?

Steve:
When do I feel strong? When I am happy with myself. Physical outlook, that is.

Evangelita:
If you can say something very angry, do you feel strong and get pleasure from it?

Steve:
Sometimes.

Evangelita:
Okay, that is the bad side that says "tut, tut," and then you can have pleasure, too, from honoring things; but that is the hard, long, road when you take your time with things. Do you miss your dad?

Steve:
(Nods no)

Evangelita:
Where is he?

Steve:
He is at home.

Evangelita:
Do you hardly see him?

Steve:
I see him, but we are not close, though.

Evangelita:
Do you miss him?

Steve:
Not really, unless I haven't seen him in a while, I do.

Evangelita:
You don't get along with him?

Steve:
We hardly speak. We get along, but we're not enemies.

Evangelita:
Do you wish you were friends with him? When was the last time you hugged him?

Steve:
When I came back from the service. When I came back from the marines.

Evangelita:
How long were you gone?

Steve:
It was over a year. I hugged him the day I left, and each time I came and left the military, I hugged everybody.

Evangelita:
You don't think he loves you?

Steve:
(Nods yes)

Evangelita:
Do you think he does or he doesn't?

Steve:
Yes.

Evangelita:
So how come you are not close?

Steve:
My mom says because we are too much alike.

Evangelita:
What is his biggest criticism of you?

Steve:
I don't know. I guess we are alike in certain ways.

Evangelita:
Does he like spaghetti?

Steve:
No, not too much.

Evangelita:
What does he like to eat?

Steve:
Gumbo.

Evangelita:
Do you?

Steve:
It's alright.

Evangelita:
You don't like it?

Steve:
I like it, but I'll eat my baked chicken, fish, baked potatoes, vegetables.

Evangelita:
So when your mother cooks, who does she cook for?

Steve:
She cooks for everybody.

Evangelita:
But I mean, who does she want to please?

Steve:
The whole family, but ...

Dr. Okun:
Is there more gumbo or baked chicken?

Steve:
I eat gumbo, but she cooks everything kinda to suit everyone.

Evangelita:
How does she manage that? Who does she want to please most?

Steve:
I wouldn't say me the most, everybody likes to eat what she prepares.

Evangelita:
But who is special to her?

Steve:
Everyone.

Evangelita:
Are you being honest now?

Steve:
I think so.

Evangelita:
So when was the last time she made gumbo?

Steve:
A few weeks ago.

Evangelita:
A few weeks ago, so what has she been cooking lately?

Steve:
Baked chicken.

Evangelita:
Okay, so she does make a lot of chicken for you?

Steve:
Chicken in some ways which everybody likes, I wouldn't say she does it for me. She tries to make healthy recipes that are less greasy.

Evangelita:
Does your father smoke?

Steve:
No, he doesn't smoke.

Evangelita:
Does he drink?

Steve:
No.

Evangelita:
Perfect.

Steve:
I wouldn't say that. I don't drink, either, but I am far from perfect.

Evangelita:
It sounds like a very healthy, happy family to me.

Steve:
Oh, the problems I have, has nothing to do with the family.

Evangelita:
What does it have to do with?

Steve:
Me.

Evangelita:
God strengthen you to bear yourself, the heaviest weight of all to bear.

Steve:
I can't blame anybody else.

Evangelita:
And what is your problem?

Steve:
How I look upon myself, I guess.

Evangelita:
And how you see the world, that is why the book is called *Self* and *World;* and confusion is right next to clearness. Do you feel less confused now than you did when you first walked in here?

Steve:
A little bit.

Evangelita:
So your confusion hasn't left?

Steve:
Not totally. To some degree.

Evangelita:
But you have more clearness on your side.

Steve:
Right.

Evangelita:
Do you know what kills the herpes virus?

Steve:
Total clearness.

Evangelita:
Light, which is clearness. Do you know that if the herpes virus stays outside of our body, it is dead. Light kills it, exposure. See, the more you come out and talk about it because it is inside of you, the less ashamed you are going to be, because it's all secret stuff.

Steve:
I have a lot of rage that gets inside of me.

Evangelita:
At whom? Do you know?

Steve:
At me.

Evangelita:
Because you are not perfect?

Steve:
I am not perfect, that's why I should be better than what I am.

Evangelita:
So, is that a reason to be angry at yourself?

Steve:
No.

Evangelita:
That is a reason to congratulate yourself.

Steve:
I know it's not right, but that is the way I have been for a long time.

Evangelita:
So, have you been too harsh with yourself? And then too lean.
We go one way or the other, but all the time we are trying to
put the opposites together; you are either flattering yourself or
cursing yourself, and when you are cursing yourself you forgot
you ever flattered yourself. Why? You shouldn't. Your good
qualities should not go away because you did something
wrong. Try integration, and that is what the virus does, it
disintegrates you constantly, only one side is honored, the
hidden side. Where is light, where is the sunny Steve, that likes
to smell the flowers? When you are in the dark doldrums, you
want to have tears. You want to die. You said you were
thinking about death lately? Believe me, that is not going to go
away, that death feeling, because it is part of you, as happy as
you are, and even if your whole face clears, and you have no
problem, it doesn't mean that you don't still have the dark
side, because then you wouldn't be all of you. It is what you are
honoring. Okay, it is like you take your hand, and you open up
your hand, let's say this is you happy (closed fist), this is you
sad (open hand), but you forgot when you are sad that you
ever had a happy side. Now I am going to be sad for five days,
you know, and now I am going to be happy for another five
days, and instead of seeing that is one hand, having different
moods, your happy mood, then your sad mood, but you are
still you, you are trying to handle all these moods, how many
moods?

Steve:
I'd have bad mood swings.

Evangelita:
Yes, if you have a dream that you are beating your girlfriend,
you see, that is a beautiful dream, in a way, because you are

being critical of yourself. In other words you don't look good to yourself, do you? You are worried about it. You are concerned and that is good, you see. If you were hitting somebody and you just felt that is the way it should be, there is something wrong with you. If I see myself acting bad, or wrongly, and I disapprove of myself, that is wonderful, there is nothing to be ashamed of. You have good stuff going on inside of you but you don't know how to applaud yourself, instead of approving of yourself, you slap yourself because you are confused. Because we needed to learn this. We all did, from Aesthetic Realism and Eli Siegel. He is the only one that made sense of the opposites. We want to punch ourselves all the time, tear ourselves, it doesn't make sense, I can't stand myself, o my God what a fool I was, I can't stand myself, I lock the door. I don't want to talk to anybody. You go through that, to the extremes, but if you can remember there's one person all the time trying to put together different parts of himself, you are going to have that herpes disappear. It won't come back.

Dr. Okun:
You will have the integration, and that is what is going to boost your immunity system up.

Evangelita:
And you won't welcome the enemy, because the enemy fools you. Don't let yourself fool you and the enemy is in you so don't let yourself fool you.

Steve:
I hope it works.

Dr. Okun:
Let me give you a couple of assignments to do. The most important thing is to keep a log, like in a notebook or on a piece of paper. Note down when you are having an outbreak, when it is getting better, when it is getting worse, the important thing is to relate that either to whom you speak to, or to whom you have to do with; even like several weeks before, you might have gotten an outbreak and it might have gotten worse—relate that outbreak to whom you are having to do with, anybody that made you very, very angry.

Steve:
Write what's the cause?

Dr. Okun:
Exactly, link it, anybody that boosted you up, anybody that humiliated you.

Evangelita:
Like who complimented you today?

Steve:
No one.

Evangelita:
Did you compliment yourself?

Steve:
I had no reason to compliment myself.

Evangelita:
Did you curse yourself? You didn't talk to yourself today? Keep track of what you tell yourself, and write it down, because that is how you know what you are telling yourself. We make it all

unconscious, we don't want to know ourselves; therefore, we don't want to listen, but because we are not listening, it doesn't mean it is not there. Find out what dialogues you have with yourself, you will be very surprised.

Dr. Okun:
Write it down. The act of writing it down is very important.

Evangelita:
The greatest monologue of all is the Shakespeare monologue from Hamlet "To be or not to be," because that is what we do every day. Shall I deal with my questions today, or shall I throw them away, sweep them all under the rug, and in the meantime you pick up the rug and they are all there.

Steve:
Collected.

Evangelita:
We use our questions to hate ourselves. So when you are having the outbreak relate that to who you are speaking to, anyone who made you angry that day.

Dr. Okun:
Or who made a lot of you or humiliated you.

Evangelita:
It could be the same person.

Dr. Okun:
Sometimes it is the same person who can put you down and make you angry and also in some way boost your ego up, and in some way bring out this contempt we're talking about. You may have a thought that this person is stupid or stupid about

you, like we said. They are boosting you up and at the same time putting you down in some way. Keep track of this in terms of physical symptoms.

Evangelita:
And relate it to the way the virus is—the virus fools the healthy cell, it gets in there and takes over, and from that day on, forget it.

Dr. Okun:
The other thing is, has the same person been smiling in front of your face, or via the telephone telling you certain things and stabbing you in the back?

Steve:
I have that a lot.

Evangelita:
If you can track it down, that will be the saving grace.

Steve:
That is true about the persons I work with, I no longer work with them, but I'm sure I will run across a new person sooner or later that will do that again.

Evangelita:
We are more like the herpes virus than different, we have the exact same qualities the herpes virus has, unless we look at that, and then see what it causes. Do you know all the viruses, like cancer, they all do the same thing?

Dr. Okun:
If you look at the structure of the cell—we have studied it in the cancer cell.

Steve:
They exist naturally.

Dr. Okun:
If you look at a cancer cell in comparison to a normal cell, they get what they called bizarre looking, they are not normal, they normally have what is called growth inhibition, where a cell will only grow so large. A cancer cell won't stop growing. That is what happens in cancer, the cancer cell has its way. It gets as large as it wants to, it piles on top of another cell, and that is how you get tumors, the cancer cell totally has its way. The same thing with the herpes virus I or II. You look at the virus microscopically: they become what they call giant cells with many nucleuses within the cell. When they took a scraping from your blister and looked at it under the microscope, something called a Tzanck prep, which is a preparation used to diagnose herpes, if you look at that cell, it is what they call a giant cell; the same thing that causes the herpes outbreaks is related to cancer and is related to the virus.

Evangelita:
And it is all blowing itself out of proportion, the cell gets humongous in having its way, that is what the herpes virus does, it becomes so important, is so conceited, that it forgets the humility part of it.

Dr. Okun:
I tell you it can happen so fast, it can happen before you know it. Someone has an effect on you and sits smiling to your face and stabs you in the back; you may not express your anger, you have that rage boiling up in there, you may feel angry, like throwing something at them, but you don't express this,

especially to a boss, or someone that has some of kind of power over you.

Evangelita:
And the purpose is, to look at this person: they think they are fooling me, I know what they do, but there is nothing I can do. Why not? There is something you can do: don't imitate them— because we do the same thing, once you start looking at yourself. Once you study begil and we call evil, begil, then you know what is good, if you study good then you know what is not good, nobody is just good and nobody is just bad. You have to relate the two, the viruses are in the same world with carnations. Can you think of a sentence with carnation and herpes virus and Potpourri? Can you make a sentence with all three things?

Steve:
All three together?

Evangelita:
Yes ...

Conclusion and Beginning

What you have just read saved Steve's life, stopped his outbreaks, and has allowed him to rise out of the depression, no longer wanting to die, and get out of his deathbed and now work two jobs.

Steve is now going into a respiratory technician program that lasts eighteen months and will give him a stable, respectable career.

Steve is now going to get married and is even expecting a new baby.

Steve did a lot of work on himself. This is what you need to do to be well yourself. You need to look at what works in you, what is good about you and not good about you, and who and what brings out your outbreaks and why you allow it to be. Why do you allow yourself to be humiliated, while praised in some subtle way? Why do you take insults? Is it a desire for money? praise? fear? A pleasure of contempt, which Steve learned about, and which makes all of us weak and sick. Do not wait until you have a painful outbreak to see what is amiss in yourself. The only way you can stay well and avoid outbreaks is by looking for criticism and not excuses.

Congratulations on knowing yourself, and remember, as Eli Siegel said, "No self can truly know itself and be ashamed."

CHAPTER 3:
Transcript of a Consultation Session with Sabrina

S abrina had been taking Zovirax twice or three times a day; when we saw her, she was only taking a pill a day. When she had an outbreak, she felt a tingling sensation or pain in the area where she had her first outbreak.

She had been diagnosed with Herpes II by culture seven months before. She had suffered from cold sores in her mouth before she began to have outbreaks of genital herpes. She was having an outbreak when we spoke to her, and her outbreak had begun two weeks earlier.

She said this attack was mild and that she had taken Zovirax for it but that the blisters had migrated to her anus and that she was having a lot more pain because the blisters became ulcerated in the area where she had her first outbreak. She was getting pain in the lower back that went into the back of her legs. She said that she had called a hotline to get more information because she was taking Zovirax around the time of her cycle but still having outbreaks in this new spot. She said that she was under increased stress because she was divorced and had children.

Sabrina:
I think the person wants to sing what is inside of them.

Evangelita:
Do you think there is an artistic way to present what is sad inside of you and then a no-good way? For example, if you are sad because someone took your money and fooled you, are you going to sit there and sing a nice melody, or are you going to write about that SOB on music sheets and say, you dirty ...

Sabrina:
(Laughs)

Evangelita:
... stinking pig, I'll get you.

Sabrina:
I think I would do it in an artistic way.

Evangelita:
Every single artist in the world that could take the patience to sit there and say "I have been fooled, I have been hurt" they have had every feeling they sing about, believe me, otherwise you would not like them. You wouldn't feel related to them. They are going to sit there, they are going to compose a song how so and so hurt them, this is art. This is what we can do with the herpes virus. You can't sit there and curse whoever gave it to you, you can't sit there and curse whoever gave it to you, you have to be an artist and you can be. It is exactly the point to this consultation; and if you study your tape you are going to get to be an artist on what gives you pain, and you are going to give yourself hope rather than doom. You won't just drop into the gutter. That is the whole purpose of this consultation, and these questions can lead you to the artistic way of seeing something, rather than the bad way of seeing something.

Sabrina:

Well, I mean, I went through a period where I felt frustrated, I didn't hate the guy, you know, he was a pretty decent person; all people have a good and a bad side. He said he didn't know that he had this, which I kind of have to doubt. He said, "My wife did at one time mention it." So I feel in that aspect of it, he did betray me, he disrespected me then, but on the other side of the coin, I am angry at myself for not taking the proper preventive measures, for my own self and putting that responsibility on somebody else's hand. So I was angry with him and was angry with myself. Then I went through this phase where I was just really depressed at having something I can't ever get rid of, and I will have it for life and it can come back every now and then, and I'll get angry about it and I'll say it is pretty much a moot point. There is no point getting angry about it. You can do something about it, but you can't get rid of it. So just try to deal with it. The problem for me now is that I either avoid relationships, or if I am in one, I am very wary about it, I am nervous about it, because I know that I have this, and you know this and you know if you tell somebody like the last guy that I dated, I thought he had feelings for me, but he really was not committed to me, to the relationship, because he was a musician, and musicians are a different sort of people. If they like you they are not going to spend that much time with you, because they will tell you that their music is the important thing, but you know I've had some problems, "Should I tell him or should I not?" And I read the little brochure saying yes, you should tell your partner, so I hedged about it, and I debated it and I agonized over it, and I said if it was me I would want to know. So I confided to him and he didn't like get all upset, and I didn't know how to take his reaction which was like, "Oh well, what can I do about it," but it was like shortly after I might have seen him once and he was history.

So, after that, I feel like, well, I am not going to tell the next person. I might take precautions about making sure that I am not exposing him, but I don't feel like I want to tell anybody. It was his choice and his right to say I don't want to take the risk, but I think it was the way he handled the whole thing. He could have said, "I don't feel comfortable seeing you again" but he didn't do that. He pretty much dumped the whole thing and walked.

Evangelita:
You can actually test how much someone loves you then. That man is not looking for love. There are some people who are not looking for love, and they will find whatever excuse they can find to be history for you. You already set him up to be someone for whom music was first; if he puts music first, nobody would be married, nobody would have children. That's ridiculous, music first. When you were around, too? You listened to him, the unfortunate thing is that you probably made him as an example. You shouldn't do that again, because your goal is to be an honest person. You don't want to be tricking people. I respect you for saying, "If it was me, I would want to be told." By the same token when one person goes off knowing what you have and you never see them again, it is a slap in your face. That is not good, that is not the answer. I agree with you. What is the answer? Okay, I will tell you what the answer is, you can actually use this ... to say "No, I will, not be dumb, I will not tell anybody unless I think they really care, until I know they love me."

Sabrina:
Why should I go risk my getting stepped on?

Evangelita:
Exactly, so you get even more cynical. No, you don't have to expose yourself like that. If you know what you are looking for, and you will find out from this consultation what you want. Once you know what you want, you get it, right, now you don't know what you want. You don't, do you? What do you want from a man?

Sabrina:
A friend of mine asked me that question several weeks ago, and I thought I knew, but I honestly could not answer, and if I can't answer this off the top of my head, then obviously I don't really know.

Evangelita:
So we are going to use this consultation to know more what you want. You can't rush your questions because they are ethical and they are beautiful. You should love your questions. That is the only way, and we will think more about this. We have prepared some questions for you.

Dr. Okun:
What do you hate the most in this world?

Sabrina:
I have to say injustice, hate seeing a person put another person down, because of whatever personal problems they have.

Evangelita:
Do you think by the same token there are some people who should be punished?

Sabrina:
Well, that is kind of a deep question. I think sometimes you do things in life in order to learn certain lessons—even with this herpes, I feel this came around to teach me something about myself, what I should be doing or not doing, so I think if a person does something, it comes back to them, and that sometimes is a punishment in itself.

Evangelita:
So you feel as far as saying you did this, so you should be locked up or whatever?

Sabrina:
Well, yes, in some extreme cases, say you go out and kill someone you know, yes, sure, you don't want this person walking around the streets until they understand why they did what they did, or show some remorse for it.

Evangelita:
So there should be punishment for those who need to be punished, and there should be no punishment for those who should not be punished. That is what you are talking about. That is what we all want. Justice ... That is what justice is, justice is not kissing a murderer, no it is not, and sometimes you think there is no justice because so many people get away with so much. Then it means there is no justice because of that, because so many people every single day get away with so much. They don't get away with it anyway, but we are made to think by the press, by the way things are covered up, that there are some people who get away with everything, and here we are and we can't get away with anything. But it isn't true, like, they give you a soap job in the press, believe it or not.

Sabrina:

Oh, I know, I was mishandled by the press.

Dr. Okun:

You were mishandled by the press?

Sabrina:

Oh, it is one of those soap opera type stories, you don't want to hear this at all, do you? Well, a few years ago, my husband and I were, our relationship was, on the rocks, and I separated from him because he was unfaithful and was not spending time like he should at home; and about this time I started therapy, and I met a real nice person, trying to help me. Someone I could talk to, so the relationship after I separated from him got more involved, but my ex-husband, he is strange, all of a sudden he decided that he really wanted me, once I am gone, so he started to stalk me and follow me. The relationship with this other person I didn't think should continue, even though we were good friends, we are still friends. So once, on one occasion after my husband coerced me to come back home because he was making me so miserable away from home, I figured I might as well be home if I am going to be miserable away from home. And one Saturday I went to work out at the health club, which was not too far from where this person lived, so I dropped over afterwards to talk to him, and his daughter said he was watching football. So apparently my husband came over, thinking that I was there, brought our son who was much smaller then, and a confrontation came about when I went outside. I just wanted to go ahead and leave because it was getting to be kind of ugly. This other person was ... I don't want to stereotype ... he kind of got frustrated with him also because my husband was threatening him and calling him and hanging up before this all happened, all kinds of stuff, so he was kind of like, "I have had it up to here," so when he escorted me out to my car, my husband walked up and tried to put himself right there in my face and that is when it got kind of rough, nobody got hurt but ... it got to be in the newspapers. But the way they wrote it up, it was humiliating because they made it look like, I am a slutty woman who is sleeping around on her husband. And at work people read it, and it was like, you have to walk in the next week, and people who I knew had read this probably put their own judgement on me by having read this, one person asked me about this, and it made me feel terrible. And the way it happened, and the way the press wrote about it was totally different. The press wrote the whole thing to make the thing titillating.

Evangelita:
They want the paper to sell, so they do it that way.

Sabrina:
But how they handled the whole thing, it was really traumatic for me because I am a very private type person. I don't have many friends, I have people that I talk to, but as far as persons to confide in, I don't. And I don't really like for my personal life to be out so for the whole world, the whole town to see that.

Evangelita:
How long ago was that?

Sabrina:
A few years ago. That was traumatic for me.

Evangelita:
And where is he now?

Sabrina:
We eventually divorced, we kind of went back and forth in our relationship.

Evangelita:
Does he have any children?

Sabrina:
That is his son. He keeps them actually during the week, and I have them on the weekends.

Evangelita:
You are in a close relationship, in close contact with him?

Sabrina:
Well, I prefer not to be. I would prefer not to be but he keeps them because he thinks I expose them to so many different people, which I don't. And he has this idea that I am sleeping with everyone in town.

Evangelita:
Did you get the herpes before you met him?

Sabrina:
No, after the divorce, well actually, he served me with papers in February of last year. The divorce was final soon after.

Dr. Okun:
So they diagnosed you in July of 1993.

Sabrina:
He still has some emotional ties to me, I suppose, because he is constantly trying to control me, my world, my environment. I went on vacation a couple of days ago, and I called him up

and asked him to pick up Miles at the daycare for the weekend, and he was highly upset because he presumed I had gone off with another man. How dare I leave Miles with him while I go off with some other person! Even though that may not have been the case, he still likes to make my life miserable for me.

Evangelita:
Did you know him when you were a young girl?

Sabrina:
To a degree when I was in college, I was a student actually. He used to date my roommate. I never liked him at all, I don't know why I married.

Evangelita:
Did you know him when you were even younger?

Sabrina:
He didn't know me from that age. He knew me from about eighteen or nineteen years old.

Evangelita:
Did he know about you?

Sabrina:
No.

Evangelita:
Are you sure?

Sabrina:
No.

Evangelita:
Does he know your parents?

Sabrina:
Now he does, but I don't really think he knew them because he lived in the South, and I didn't grow up there. So he wouldn't have known them.

Evangelita:
Does he have brothers?

Sabrina:
Yes, he does. Well, my grandfather who raised me is dead, and my father is dead, too.

Evangelita:
Your father is dead. How old were you when he died?

Sabrina:
I was twenty-six years old, and actually my grandfather and my father both died the same year. But they never met him. This was my second marriage, no, they never met him.

Evangelita:
So you had a first marriage, and your parents did know him and what happened to him.

Sabrina:
It lasted about seven years. He was very abusive.

Evangelita:
That is the one that your parents knew, and he knew you when you were about twelve years old?

ERASING SCARS

Sabrina:
He didn't know me, either. I met him when I came down here to go to school.

Evangelita:
So who did you know when you were twelve years old? Did you ever meet an older man when you were younger?

Sabrina:
Oh, gosh, that was when I was in junior high school. My folks were very strict, I guess, when I think about it. He was a real sweet guy. It wasn't like it was a very big deal for me. I didn't mind. They really freaked because he was so much older than me. And five or seven years is a big difference when you are that young. Now, it isn't a big deal.

Evangelita:
Was he like Elvis falling in love, do you know their story?

Sabrina:
No, he was just a real nice soft-spoken person, shy and quiet.

Evangelita:
So was Elvis, too, remember he met that young girl and waited until she was of age to marry him.

Sabrina:
No, seriously, the thing that impressed me about him—I don't know why he was interested in me because I was so young.

Evangelita:
Elvis actually waited until she grew and then she married him.

Sabrina:
He was going to do that, too.

Evangelita:
Why didn't he marry you?

Sabrina:
Well, by the time I got ready to graduate from high school, I just decided that I had not seen enough—I didn't want to commit myself to a marriage. I never wanted to say after looking back "I wish I had done something else," now I think back and wished I had married the man.

Evangelita:
But didn't he get married to somebody else?

Sabrina:
Yes, I am not saying he was just and all wonderful a person. I think he has broken a couple of hearts because I have heard tales that he has had a lot of problems with alcohol and all of this.

Evangelita:
Did you ever call him up?

Sabrina:
Yes, once in a blue moon, we will see each other, maybe at church. He eventually married and has a family, and he is a deacon at church. At one time I really wished I had married him, I told him that.

Evangelita:
Does this have to do with what you want, you have to know what you want ...

Sabrina:
And I felt he was the only person, when I think back, the only one romantically-wise that really cared about me, because he never questioned me, I mean, like we never got intimate, he never pressured me, he respected that, we didn't go out on dates, unless my sister went, too. We were just ... I figured he must have loved me or something, he was going to go through all those changes, wait until I was of age, wait until I grew up. I have always compared everyone else to him. He was always with the college guys, so my folks didn't like it. But at least we got to know each other, but like I said at the time that he wanted to get married.

Evangelita:
And how long did he wait?

Sabrina:
About four years after that.

Evangelita:
That was a pretty long time; and did you think at that time you would know what you wanted?

Sabrina:
No, I really did not want to marry him, either.

Evangelita:
Who chose your wedding gown?

Sabrina:
My wedding gown was borrowed. My wedding gown belongs to my first husband's sister. I didn't even have a wedding gown, I didn't have a honeymoon.

Evangelita:
Were you pregnant?

Sabrina:
Yes, I was pregnant.

Evangelita:
How many months were you pregnant?

Sabrina:
Two or four months maybe, and I felt this intense pressure to get married because I did not want to disappoint my folks, and I think that was the whole thing for me. In retrospect I thought I didn't have a choice at that time, the urge not to disappoint my folks overpowered what I felt, that it was not going to be good for me.

Evangelita:
And who put on your wedding gown?

Sabrina:
My grandmother and some of his older sisters.

Evangelita:
Did anyone say something insulting to you?

Sabrina:
He had a girlfriend at the time and met me more on a rebound, and because he had dated this girl for years and years, everyone expected them to get married. And I remember him telling me that she had told him that he didn't have to marry me.

ERASING SCARS

Evangelita:
That is like a knife, no, he didn't have to marry you, that sounded like he was having contempt. Things will start to make sense to you as we go on with the questions.

Dr. Okun:
So who do you know that slaps you the most and then caresses you the most?

Sabrina:
He could do that, he was a master at it. But he did more slapping than caressing. But he was like that. My daughter to a degree has a lot of his personality.

Evangelita:
Does she look like him?

Sabrina:
Oh yeah, definitely, she can be that way. She is thirteen. She seems very clinging and she needs a lot of attention, a lot of attention.

Evangelita:
Are you too interested in yourself to be interested in your children?

Sabrina:
At one time I felt so.

Evangelita:
I should wear a sign myself, "I am too interested in myself to be interested in you." Mothers feel that. I have three children. It seems like everyone is always wanting something from you.

Sabrina:
I had a lot of issues going on with me, that I was trying to work through. I didn't know why I was going through all this, I was very unhappy. So I felt like, I was okay for me, so I couldn't give her anything.

Evangelita:
But do you think in having her, you gave up a lot, you gave up everything? You gave up your independence. You married someone that told you "I don't have to marry you," you got slapped. All because you had the baby, who can be a brat when she wants to be, you gave up a lot for this man. You didn't have to marry him, you could have had an abortion. You know there are a lot of girls out there that have abortions and it's like nothing, but you know they can act like it never happened because not everyone knows about it. In the meantime you know they had the abortion and they didn't have to get married. But you got married, you didn't have an abortion, and you got slapped. And he tells you, he didn't have to do it. Do you resent your position, even though you were doing the right thing? I think you did, I don't believe in abortion, do you?

Sabrina:
No, I never really thought about it.

Evangelita:
I believe it is an option and it is up to us to decide.

Sabrina:
Well, at the time, I was very idealistic, and I said, "Well if I am going to be grown up enough to have sex with this man, then I can be grown up enough to go ahead with it all."

Evangelita:
But that was your choice.

Sabrina:
In retrospect, I love my children dearly, but life could have been a lot more different, but they are here now.

Evangelita:
That is what I am saying. You can respect yourself for the choices you made, you did nothing wrong. I believe like you, I had every child, because if God gave me the chance to have my child, it seemed to me I could have not done anything else. And I wouldn't do it. And this is why I respect myself. And people can think whatever they want. That doesn't mean anything, if ten years ago you had done different, and you would not have your little girl that you love, would you have missed something?

Sabrina:
I feel like I would not have grown as a person, because I would not have reached deeper within myself, and I don't think I would have if I had not had her.

Evangelita:
Do your children keep you alive? And we mean a-l-i-v-e. Where would you be if you didn't have them, to bug you, where would you be?

Sabrina:
Probably lonely, because you know when I look at it, the relationships I have had, and I am not really comfortable with saying that, because I was looking for love, to have them love me, because I did not love myself. They have always been

there, and I am not going to sacrifice them for somebody else, because they are here with me.

Evangelita:
But I feel you have made the right choice, and you should respect yourself for that. God knows everything that you have been through, you want God to approve of you. You want God to tell you that you are okay, because no one else can tell you that. Because when you die, or are near death, he is the one you want to be with, and I know that you have been near death, were you in an accident?

Sabrina:
Well I was raped, and that day I had a sense of foreboding, but I didn't know what it was from, what it could be. But it was bad!

Evangelita:
When you have been tortured to death, do you know who it was? Was he a stranger?

Sabrina:
He was someone I knew about, that I had had lunch with, went to classes with.

Evangelita:
So by a miracle of God you are here. Did you ever press charges against him?

Sabrina:
I did, and they went through the whole investigation and locked him up and everything and waited for me to press charges against him, my family talked me out of it because

they were afraid that he would come back, once he got out of prison, to get back at me for that.

Dr. Okun:
But you were badly beaten?

Sabrina:
Oh, yeah, not really bad, but it was a point where I became unconscious.

Evangelita:
So what happens to the person that has been treated in that horrific way, that is something that he had no right to? We talked about punishment at the beginning; if someone takes a young person and does whatever they want to them, that is against God, I don't think God likes that, that is evil, having its way and saying there is no God here, I can do what I want, I am God and if I want to bury you I will. And that is the right that people give themselves, but it is not God, he can't do that and get away with that, that is horrendous, this is why we are studying the virus, because when you study the virus, you will see that it works just like these people, who think they have the right to have bad power over you, and there is no difference between the way the virus takes over you and these people. There is no difference between the guy who raped you and the virus. Because the viruses work just in the same way as the rapist did. That man killed you, the moment he put his hands on you, you were dead. Your soul was shocked out of your body, and you are like a walking corpse, after that, you are not alive, you are dead!

Sabrina:
Yes, I know, that is how I felt.

Evangelita:
Anytime something like that happens to us, our soul goes to God, and to be able to go back and re-live that moment, and then say "You, dear God, are just as angry with this man as I am," and you want people like that dead. No mother, no father can say they want that that man should not be put away; because he will go on doing it to somebody else, he did not stop with you.

Sabrina:
I know.

Evangelita:
Your parents, as scared as they were about you, they had no right to tell you not to press charges. If someone takes your daughter at nineteen and rapes her, like you were raped, you are not going to tell me you are going to let the guy go, and tell your daughter don't press charges after what happened to you? How many other people has this animal assaulted like that?

Sabrina:
Oh, I harbor some resentment against that, not being able to go forth, that is what is always in back of my mind, if he is doing this to somebody else.

Evangelita:
He has done it again, the criminal mind first of all to attack a young girl didn't start with you, God knows how many other young girls he has hurt, before you and how many after you. Nobody normal, only the criminally insane, can do that to young girls, and scare you half to death and cut your body up, yes, you have to put that man away no matter how old you are. You have to put him away, or you will never be happy.

Sabrina:
This is probably why I worked at the rape crisis center for a while.

Evangelita:
You see, you do have a big feeling about it. As an assignment, you should write exactly what happened to you that night; when you keep something so horrific like that inside, and you bring it out, and give it light, something can change; like the artist that we talked of earlier, you can give it melody because you don't have to carry around the grudge, you bring it out and give it structure, you can have it published. When you have art you are able to bring out the worst, most horrible thing that happened in your life and put it out so everyone can see it. You can say, "This happened to me when I was nineteen and I was not allowed to press charges, and I never felt good about it, and it can happen to you, and you should be able to talk about it."

CHAPTER 4:
Transcript of an Aesthetic Realism Lesson

Norma Rosenthal, aka Evangelita Goodwell, grew up in El Salvador and Guatemala and, after her family came to the United States, in New York. She was an apprentice at the Berkshire Playhouse and attended the prestigious Neighborhood Playhouse in New York City where she studied acting with Sanford Meisner, among others. She also studied with Lynn Masters at Carnegie Hall and worked in summer stock with the Allenberry Playhouse in Pennsylvania before returning to New York City in 1969.

In December 1969, she went with some students of Aesthetic Realism to see a performance of Ibsen's play *Hedda Gabler*. This particular production was being produced by the Opposites Company, under the direction of Ted van Griethuysen, with Eli Siegel as the Aesthetic Advisor. The method of acting and directing in this production, which affected Miss Rosenthal deeply, was that of Aesthetic Realism. After attending the performance, Miss Rosenthal wrote to Mr. Siegel and asked to become a student of Aesthetic Realism. She began to attend classes regularly beginning in February 1970 and continued attending classes and lessons until 1981.

The lesson which is presented in the transcript that follows took place eight months after Miss Rosenthal began to study with Mr. Siegel. The transcript demonstrates a number of the general principles of Aesthetic Realism, especially those involving ill will, contempt, and depression. Miss Rosenthal is shown dealing with deep questions about her life that Mr. Siegel addresses directly. In the transcript Miss Rosenthal tries to portray a happy, bubbling exterior, while inside she was churning emotionally and felt that she had "scraped the bottom of hopelessness." After the lesson Miss Rosenthal was able to see her disposition much more clearly, made aware by Mr. Siegel that she wanted to stand and preach from a position of ill will rather than good will. Eli Siegel sticks to his principles throughout, forcing Miss Rosenthal to "work like hell" in order to integrate her two contrasting sides and turn from "a Roman warrior into a Christian."

Subsequently, Mr. Siegel named Miss Rosenthal an Aesthetic Realism Consultant in November 1973, entitling her to teach Aesthetic Realism in English and Spanish. She has given Aesthetic Realism consultations (such as with Steve and Sabrina, in the preceding chapters) since 1973.

A few other notes for the lesson: Aesthetic Realism consultants Bertha Bania and Ken Kimmelman appear in the course of the transcript. Bertha Bania was Miss Rosenthal's roommate at the time; Ken Kimmelman was her first husband and is an animator and filmmaker in New York City. The kind of lesson that is represented in this transcript is derived from the lessons in Aesthetic Realism that Eli Siegel began to give in 1940. Aesthetic Realism developed as an outgrowth of poetry classes taught by Mr. Siegel, whose students asked him for lessons that could deal (in terms of life itself) with what on the level of poetry contributed to the beauty of a poem. Mr. Siegel's lessons took place in front of an entire class (thus the participation of several people is evidenced in the transcript). Mr. Siegel also gave classes on arts and sciences, poetry, the profit system, and others. Mr. Siegel died in November 1978.

Aesthetic Realism Lesson of
Norma Rosenthal with Eli Siegel
Sunday, 18 October 1970

Eli Siegel:
(Reads document from Norma Rosenthal)

> Dear Mr. Siegel:
>
> Today I had a feeling like the one I had at my first Communion. I feel deeply honored. I feel deeply grateful. I'm grateful to Bertha Bania for understanding criticisms. I'm also deeply grateful to Ken Kimmelman. I feel today that God is on the side of man.

Is there anything different from this you feel?

Norma Rosenthal:
I can—

ES:
I'd like to say this. The purpose of man is to find a continuous relation between good and evil without getting them mixed up. And so, when a person tells me and tells others that everything is so fine—certainly it's good to hear, but I happen not to believe it. So where not? Aesthetic Realism is a process and anybody who is perfect prematurely will get thrown out. Mr. Bonura's getting pale. (Laughter from company) Do you know what I mean by that? You like to act like a starry-eyed Catholic

girl—pardon the sectarianism—who has come upon the Virgin Mary and the Apostles at once and said she's unworthy of them but in the meantime looks rapturous. Once Miss Singer used to do that from another religious point of view—she had a way of looking rapturous. So why am I objecting to this?

NR:
Because it's not the truth.

ES:
I think your thoughts about your brother are ugly.

NR:
That's true.

ES:
Now have I introduced—. So tell me where it's good. You have another communication. What's wrong with him?

NR:
With my brother?

ES:
Your thoughts about your brother.

NR:
With my thoughts.

ES:
Also your sister. I think you have a sister, too.

NR:
Yes.

ES:
Too bad.

Bertha Bania:
Her younger brother came last night for the first time.

ES:
For instance, the person who is having the next lesson, Miss Musicant, is listening and she is watching me. I think she's a little nervous. I won't ask—this is your lesson. Still, do you like your thoughts about your brother? You can say it straight. What don't you like?

NR:
Well—

ES:
You know you had this dream. So why do you think it was that way?

NR:
Because I guess I make less of him in my mind.

ES:
No, because you act to him as if you were better then you are. That's what the dream says.

NR:
I have thought I am better than my brother.

ES:
That may be, but even if you're better, there's a certain way of acting better. For instance, I think I'm better than our

Secretary of Defense, Mr. Laird—everybody in this room, by the way, is. There's a certain way of acting better. Yes?

NR:
(Pause)

ES:
Now, Miss Rosenthal, talk about your brother so that we can get all the hearts and flowers away.

NR:
I have two.

ES:
Two brothers?

NR:
Yes.

ES:
All right, so talk about the one who was in the dream.

NR:
The one that was in the dream is one year older than I am. I don't like his ethics, for one thing.

ES:
All right.

NR:
I think that he doesn't care for people enough.

ES:

Do you like your ethics about a person whose ethics you don't like?—if you know what I mean. In other words, our way of seeing a bad person can be bad.

NR:

Because I use him to make myself better.

ES:

No. Miss Rosenthal, the purpose of an Aesthetic Realism lesson is to be encouraged to see the world better or reality better. Reality consists, as it does in painting, of three things: what is close to us, what's in the middle ground, and then what we know exists and is far off. Mr. Kimmelman and your brother are close to you. Then there are people like Mr. Reiss. You're in the middle ground, Mr. Reiss. I'm sorry, but that's the way you are. That is, you're not one of Miss Rosenthal's confidants, etc.

Daniel Reiss:

I always thought I was. (Laughter)

ES:

Then there are people of whom you've heard and read about. We try to see each one of these departments of reality: what is near, what is in the middle ground, what is distant, in the best way. Anyway, that is the purpose of Aesthetic Realism. So do you think you can see your brother in a better way?

NR:

Yes, I can.

ES:
What are you so scared of? You've got so much confidence—
what are you so scared of?

NR:
That I'll be inarticulate, and I won't say what I really feel.

ES:
Do you think you should be scared?

NR:
I don't think I should be.

ES:
If you like being scared, tell why.

NR:
I don't like being scared.

ES:
Why are you scared now? I didn't ask you to be. You admit
that?

NR:
To be scared?

ES:
What are you scared of, then? You're here to find out about
yourself. If you think everything you're going to hear is good—.
Our organization doesn't work that way.

NR:
I don't think I should be scared.

ES:

In the Catholic Church and others, there are the Cardinal Virtues, but there are also the Seven Deadly Sins. The Seven Deadly Sins haven't been wholly superseded. You think, for instance, that envy is a deadly sin. I can talk to you like a father confessor, if need be. You've gone to Confession?

NR:

Once in my life.

ES:

You should go to them more often. (Laughter)

NR:

I guess I could.

ES:

My child, hast thou ever succumbed to that sin so common even among the faithful, which is called envy? Have you ever had what that English writer called *superbia* in his translation of Chaucer—have you had haughtiness?

NR:

Yes.

ES:

Superbia. Well, it is a very common failing, my child, and neither of course try to increase it, but be not too downcast. Dost thou think that thy feeling about thy brother has given thee *superbia?* I cannot countenance it. I'd say there is hope on the subject, but I cannot of course praise you for that.

NR:

That's true.

ERASING SCARS

ES:
Shall I?

NR:
No, don't.

ES:
The using of people to be better—I'm now changing my role somewhat—is a very common thing. People are doubtful of themselves, and then they see somebody else make a mistake, or they know he's not so good, and they use the failing of another to give themselves the quality. The fact that a fifty-cent piece is more than a quarter doesn't mean that a fifty-cent piece is all of a dollar. It's still more than a quarter, but it's not everything. So this way of using people—I think you've done that with your father.

NR:
Yes, I have.

ES:
I have a notion you do it with Mr. Kimmelman. Well; after all, we all know that girls are better than men. Yes? Any girl knowing a man who doesn't think she's better, hasn't been observing. Yes?

NR:
I think you're right.

ES:
But what has this to do with your life?

NR:
I get a lot of pain from that.

ES:
So it means, then, that it's not necessary for your life?

NR:
No.

ES:
The study of our lives is the study of what obstructs and what furthers. Well, I think we took care of this *superbia*. How about *invidia?*

NR:
Same thing.

ES:
Envy. (Reads)
> "God is on the side of man. It is we who must
> know how kind and gentle his world is."

You really think that? Let's say this: it happens that Canada is perhaps as much Catholic as it is Protestant. It is Presbyterian with Scots, in one part of the country, and it is Episcopalian, to be sure, but there are also many Catholics. Now this news from Montreal, have you heard it? What do you think it says of God?

NR:
I haven't heard the news.

ES:
I'll tell you the news. They found the shot body of the Minister of Labor of Quebec; which shows that people can be angry. Anyway, since that has happened before, what do you think it says of God?

ERASING SCARS

NR:
Well, the way I see it, is that what causes a person to be against—

ES:
Do you think God wants to be called "gentle"? It is said: "God moves in mysterious ways, his wonders to perform." All right. But some of those ways are not gentle. Do you think this gentleness is sincere on your part? Do you think you're somewhere a tough baby?

NR:
Yes, I do.

ES:
Show it here. We all want to see it. All persons who want to see Miss Rosenthal show herself as a tough baby—(Unanimous show of hands) They're all interested. You don't want to?

NR:
I do, but what do I do?

ES:
It happens that the way to be a tough baby is to sometimes— did you ever curse your brother?

NR:
Oh yes.

ES:
All right, so do it again. We're all impatient. How did you curse your brother? Saying God is a gentle God? How did you curse him?

NR:
For him to go to hell and leave me alone.

ES:
Why don't you say this: I don't understand, God, why you gave me such—I won't use the word—such a ... for a brother.

NR:
I don't understand, but God gave me such a forth brother?

ES:
No, blank. Such a, blank, for a brother.

NR:
No. I don't understand, God, you gave me such a—brother.

ES:
Do you say it that way?

NR:
No.

Ken Kimmelman:
I've heard her say it another way.

ES:
What do you think of that? I don't mind your being angry. It's how well you do it. God himself says he's an angry and jealous God. You know he says that—he doesn't say he's just gentle. Yes?

NR:
Yes, I see.

ERASING SCARS

ES:
Do you like your disposition?

NR:
No.

ES:
What's wrong with it?

NR:
It's too lazy.

ES:
No, it's not just too lazy. It happens that in a disposition—which means "drift," or how we're disposed—there is such a thing as ill will. Did you ever have any of that?

NR:
Yes.

ES:
Now Miss Rosenthal, have you heard me use that word before?

NR:
Yes, I have. (Laughs)

ES:
What are you so surprised at?

NR:
I do have ill will.

ES:
All right, so what do you think of it?

NR:
I don't like it.

ES:
Miss Carpenter, I have heard the Catholic church is quite clearly against ill will.

Margot Carpenter:
It tries to be, yes. It doesn't always know what it's against, but it says it is.

ES:
That's right. And there are many writings against it. I have met some myself. So this happens to be as deep a sin as any: the thinking that our attitude to our brethren and our sisters is not so good, it is ill-disposed. Do you think an ill disposition is the same as ill will?

NR:
It's in me?

ES:
An ill disposition?

NR:
Yes.

ES:
Do you feel that when you're against yourself, do you think that is one of the reasons that you think so?

NR:
I don't think that's one of the reasons that I think.

ES:
This is what I mean. People get very depressed. Aesthetic Realism says that, while bad luck may cause depression, the other thing is they don't like the way their mind works—these people who are depressed. They feel that what works in them doesn't look so good to them. For instance, do you think that if a person is mean, it will make him more depressed or less depressed?

NR:
More depressed.

ES:
Then it's possible that if you have ill will—because being mean and having ill will are quite the same thing—do you think that has helped to get you down?

NR:
Yes.

ES:
Isn't it, then, good to know about it?

NR:
Yes.

ES:
And to see as much about it as possible? Do you think that is what makes you frightened now?

NR:
I'm not quite sure.

ES:

Let's say this: I think I have good will to you. If I don't, I should listen to the same criticism. Do you feel you have nothing but good will to people here and to me?

NR:

No, I don't feel that way.

ES:

Do you think that makes you frightened? I see this: there are two things that make people ashamed. One is their hope not to respect me, and the other is ill will. That goes for everybody here. I've never yet seen anybody say: "I've just cashed in on some unwillingness to respect, or ill will."

NR:

You asked me if I thought—

ES:

Do you think you have some ill will to me?

NR:

Yes, I do.

ES:

Do you believe that makes you frightened?

NR:

It does make me frightened.

ES:

It's a good thing to know.

Ellen Reiss:
What is the difference between the unwillingness to respect and the ill will?

ES:
Ill will is usually thought of in terms of what you want to have happen to a person. That is, whether you want that person to be happy or not. Ill will takes in two things: one is the desire to disrespect, and the other is to have misfortune. For instance, if there was a terrific review against the Williams-Siegel Documentary or something else, people would have a disposition to enjoy it a little. That would be both aspects of ill will: one, the feeling that it wasn't too pleasing, and the other that they had a chance for less respect. Anyway, I don't trust anybody wholly on the subject. Yes?

Barbara Singer:
Are we frightened because we are afraid something bad will come out of us?

ES:
We're frightened because if we don't like the way we see a person, then we can show our sheepishness. I think that can be. If our intention with a person, our hopes about a person, are not the best, we can show our ill-at-easeness.

Therefore, I recommend that everybody be proud of their hopes. I think in the instance of Miss Rosenthal, she thinks she ought to have nothing but good wishes, nothing but respect, but she finds a few sinuous things of disrespect and not such good wishes. That makes you ill at ease with yourself. It has with others. I remember I mentioned that Nat Herz showed that. Very often he was very uneasy with me. He would wriggle a little bit like Uriah Heep and some other people. The reason was—I'm sure that this goes on everywhere here. I also say this: will you please look at it? Your ill will, though you don't see it, makes you ashamed. Ill will is the cause of depression. I'm trying, what with the Profit System and all, to show that good will and ill will actually exist and are not just the pastors darlings. Yes?

NR:
I like what you're saying very much.

ES:
No, you don't wholly like it yet, Miss Rosenthal.

NR:
But I like to listen.

ES:
All right, you can listen. But the purpose of this lesson is to say: I like myself more and I like the way I see the world more; and because I like the way I see the world more, I think I'm in a better relation with the world. Do you feel you're adopting the attitude of a resigned sinner now, with your hands folded? Cut it out, it's boring. Yes. "Yes, father, I shall try to amend, father. Yes, this comes home to my bosom, father." Cut it out! The one difference between Aesthetic Realism and certain agencies of divine ministry is that Aesthetic Realism gives you the chance to argue and ask "what do you mean?" and to be logical. If you are confessing your sins, a father feels that he has to point out a few sins, and you behave, and you go home refreshed.

Devorah Tarrow:
I was thinking it might be useful for Miss Rosenthal to say where she thinks she has good will, say, for her brother, and state her opinion.

ES:
Yes, certainly. I think that I implied that. It isn't a matter of good will. I say that Miss Rosenthal doesn't like the way she sees her brother and doesn't give him a right to be critical of her. She thinks she has the right to be critical of him. Does he have the right to be critical of you? Or is he so stupid he has no such right?

NR:
I think he's so stupid he has no right.

ES:
Yes; do you think God agrees with you?

NR:
No, I think God disagrees with me.

ES:
Even a turtle has a right to be critical of us, and sometimes is. (Reads note)

> "Miss Baird—I understand that Norma told Roy Harris she had chosen despair Thursday night. I think this might be useful for Mr. Siegel to know."

So what about this?

NR:
When I got out of work I wanted to go home. I didn't want to talk to anybody. I wanted just to be alone.

ES:
Why? Does that mean you like Aesthetic Realism? (NR pauses) Look, Miss Rosenthal, I don't think anybody wholly likes what I tell them. I never pretended it. I do think, however, that with honest discussion, people can like what they heard more. I think sometimes you get tired of Aesthetic Realism, and you're very angry with it. This is one of the reasons for Thursday night. Do you think that is true?

NR:
Yes, it must be true, because I do that.

ES:
It's for you to see. You act as if you had just one possibility. It happens that things can go wrong or not too clearly, and suddenly one is against Aesthetic Realism and the students of Aesthetic Realism. It happens so often. What do you think, Mr. Spears? Do you think it could happen?

Harvey Spears:
Yes.

ES:
And does it happen! You're ashamed of yourself for that, which is good. For instance, Miss Carpenter said yesterday that she didn't like the way she was angry last year about this time. It was a good thing for her to say. But at the same time, she admitted she was angry. Now do you feel that you wholly like taking orders from me? I want to put it bluntly, because

that's the way it's changed. You listen to a person; it's about your life, and you change it into taking orders. What do you think, Mr. Carduner?

Jeffrey Carduner:
You change it into taking orders.

ES:
That's right. I took the good yacht, Carduner, and told it it should go this way. Yes? (NR Pauses) Look, are you a peppy, independent señorita?

NR:
Yes.

ES:
Why don't you show it here? Do you like taking orders?

NR:
No.

ES:
Do you think in a way I give you orders?

NR:
Yes, I guess so.

ES:
Well, I did. The terrible order I give to a person is: Why in hell don't you know yourself better? Go ahead, get to work. I think it's very insulting. Also, I tell a person I'm saying this, and I think you should think about it. For instance, here, I give you this order, Norma Rosenthal: Think about what you heard. Hear! Otherwise we have a way of dealing with such people

who don't want to think about what they heard! (Laughter) Well, I have the following note:

> "Martha, I feel Mr. Siegel should know these facts. From what I have seen, what angered her family most was when she pushed things to them. She never wants to take time to listen to them."

Do you believe then that you were an indignant evangelist?

NR:
Indignant?

ES:
This is what I mean: there's a way of telling people what to do. For instance, "Irene Reiss, there are a few things you should take care of, but quick. I'm not going to say this again." Now, do you believe you like to have that manner?

NR:
Yes.

ES:
To tell a person off.

NR:
It is familiar.

ES:
All right, but what do you think of it? There is a way of being critical. It is not easy, because most people, when they're critical, are offensive. I'm critical; I try not to be offensive, but I think sometimes I have been. I don't want to say that every

time goes well. Do you feel that you want to lay down the law, you want to be a sort of Norma John the Baptist?

NR:
I feel that way.

ES:
Are you worthy of that?

NR:
Am I what?

ES:
Are you worthy of that?

NR:
Not yet.

ES:
For instance: The time of repentance is at hand, family. I'm telling you this. The hour glass is falling. So you like to do that?

NR:
Yes.

ES:
What do you think of that? Do you think it makes you pleased with yourself?

NR:
I don't think so. No.

ES:

We all like to lay down the law to someone. We get a little consolation in life making another person feel bad. Do you like to minister reproof to people?

NR:

Maybe I like it so much.

ES:

Administer reproof or minister reproof to people—either way is useful. Would you like to scold everybody? Would you say to Mrs. Mellon, "Why in hell don't you do better?" Go ahead.

NR:

Why in hell don't you do better?

ES:

That's too mild. (Company agrees) Don't you want to say it more strongly?

KK:

She can say it better than that.

MC:

I've heard Miss Rosenthal scold almost everyone I've ever seen her with, including myself.

ES:

It's good to scold in a way. Scold is related to criticism. But again, there's the motive. What motive do you have? Right now you should be very sharp. I'm scolding you. I'm giving you hell. I ain't said a nice thing now for years. What is the motive?

NR:
To have me be better.

ES:
If it isn't that, you shouldn't listen.

NR:
Sure, that's what it is.

ES:
I'm not sure—but still, if it isn't that, you should not listen. Anybody who dares to criticize a person and doesn't take care of the motive is a slob and a low person and shouldn't have been born. At the same time, being born we have to take it. More than ever, if you're going to make a person feel uncomfortable, the reason they feel uncomfortable should make for something. That is, it should be valuable. To make a person uncomfortable and not to have a good motive is two crimes at once. It's like a poem that Miss de Gomar translated, "Poem of Subtle Duality." I said there were two goods at once there, which is a little subtle. If you're going to make a person feel bad and your motive is not something good, then there are two evils at once. Do you see that? When you criticize people do you like yourself for why?

NR:
Sometimes I do.

ES:
In other words, you're uncertain on the subject.

NR:
Yes, I'm uncertain. I have felt sometimes when I am critical of Ken—

ES:
We're talking now of your whole life.

NR:
Of my whole life?

ES:
I think your motive in criticizing your father, your two brothers, and your sister could be better.

NR:
I do, too. I want it to be better.

ES:
All right, so how is it going to be better?

NR:
My motives changing.

ES:
There was once a man. A car came to his filling station. The driver of the car said, "There is something wrong with this. Will you look it over?" The man then honestly said, "I don't know what's wrong with the car, and therefore I cannot mend it." If you want to go and help somebody, you have to be sure about what is amiss. Do you follow?

NR:
Yes.

ES:
That should be seen calmly. In the mechanical field, most often one can see it. Very often a person doesn't know what's wrong and does something that's a little lucky, and it helps the

car anyway. However, in the field of ethics, it's very important to see clearly what is amiss. If a person feels I'm not trying to say it clearly, they should object. When that father confessor was talking earlier, he was as clear as he could be, everything considered. But here again, I would say that there is a certain joy which is hurtful to the person having it in finding something amiss with other people. That has been a frequent thing. Every time we have a bad motive and use it, it gets back to ourselves and hurts us.

ER:
What is the relation between Miss Rosenthal's hurtful joy in the way she's critical and wanting to make things seem so sweet?

ES:
I think that Miss Rosenthal has a sense somewhere that she has been too harsh, not careful enough in what she has seen wrong with people. As usual, there's action and reaction. And so, it's a little bit like an orchestra, after playing rock and roll it plays some stringed music. Anyway, there's such a tendency. Do you believe you get away from the fact that you can be quite sharp?

NR:
Yes.

ES:
You go from something sharp in music to stringed instruments.

NR:
Yes.

ES:

What do you think of that? Everyone can do that. Everyone here has insulted people and been harsh and they've been ashamed of it. The only thing is that persons are not as honest as they should be about it. The phrase that should go on in everybody is: I'm sorry, dear, for what I haven't said yet." Get that motto, Irene Reiss: "I'm sorry, dear, for what I haven't said yet." Yes?

NR:

I feel that—

ES:

Do you want to take the motto from Mrs. Reiss? I'm sorry, dear, for what I haven't said yet.

NR:

No. I don't like that.

ES:

Do you believe you're itching to say something of a harsh nature to people?

NR:

But if it's not going to bring me joy, I don't want it.

ES:

I'm just asking—after all.

NR:

Something that would be—

ES:
Miss Rosenthal, may I remind you that we're working? We're working.

NR:
I know.

ES:
Yes? I feel that I can, if a person wants me to, make clearer and clearer what that person has against himself or herself. That is what I'm trying to do. I feel that sometimes you think you're a mean person, and you don't have enough love in your heart, and you never will have the kind of love you want to have. It's a way Mr. Bonura has felt and others. For this to be explained needs some real listening. Do you follow?

NR:
Yes.

ES:
If a person wants to see, I think that can be—the person will see. It happens that in this world persons don't wholly want to see. Do you think you're capable of all the love you'd like to have?

NR:
Would I have felt that what?

ES:
Are you capable of all the love you'd like to have?

NR:
Yes, I am.

ES:
You're capable? Do you think there's anything in the way?

NR:
Yes.

ES:
What's in the way?

NR:
Resentment.

ES:
Let's not talk ... What do you think is in the way? I may say that Miss Musicant has a list of opposites in her letter. I'll talk about that. Let's assume that everybody in this room has two pleasures: one, "Oh you're so kind to me, dear," and "I knew all along that I was being deceived by you, you yap." Do you think both pleasures are in people that way?

NR:
Uh huh.

ES:
Do you think, then, that your desire to be deceived and your desire to see something wrong is against your desire to love? Nobody can love who cannot bring together their skepticism, their cynicism, their desire to hate and make a one with it. Otherwise, you just might as well give up, because all the energy of hate, cynicism, contempt, must go for love, otherwise, what you're going to have is wished-for collision. The car of love will be going along and then there's something very attractive: this is my time to be cynical. It gets in the way. Do you understand? It is possible to be keen. But usually when

people are critical, there's malice. As soon as you have malice, you're not a critic; you're just a hurt person. So do you think you're a good critic?

NR:
No.

ES:
No person who is a bad critic can ever love. I said that in part of the article on Barnes and Kerr which was printed.* I said that the chief reason for being a bad critic is ill will. Some persons may remember that. Also, the chief reason for not being able to love is a certain secret pleasure in ill will which gets in the way, and the feeling that you cannot be critical unless you have ill will. If that's so, then everybody would have to love fractionally. You have to be in two businesses. That is, you're in the ill will business and the love business. But it happens that one can be critical in love, but not have ill will in love—that's impossible. Those two, as sometimes opposites, they don't mix. For instance, a bottle of milk and a trombone are opposites. If you get the bottle of milk into the trombone, the trombone doesn't play so well. Do you believe that you have two desires: one to love people and the other to tell them off?

* "Two Critics of the New Hedda Gabler" by Eli Siegel. *New York Times,* Sunday, 15 March 1970, Section 2, p. 3

NR:
(Laughs and nods yes)

ES:

All right. You cannot make opposites one until they are placed truly. The desire to be critical of people and the desire to love can make a one. But the desire to tell off and the desire to love come from the top, not from the beginning. All opposites, when they are one, are seen that way at the beginning of things. Then they are related to what's going on.

HS:

What do you mean by the beginning of things?

ES:

This is what I mean. A person at the beginning of things welcomes the world and also questions it right at the beginning. The desire to question it is part of the desire to welcome. That is, the reason that a good critic questions music is because he wants to have a deeper feeling for it. But later he says he's a critic, but his desire is to tell something off. For instance, I say Barnes and Kerr are not critics because their desire was to show me up right from the beginning. They didn't want to put together their desire to see something good and their desire to see something lacking. If you can't be deep, you have to be a mess. The idea of being deep is to bring the depth to what is going on. So the thing, then, is this: Do you believe you had a big fight? The way at the moment I'm seeing what a question is for you: you would like to love something, but it's hard for you to believe that, when you love something, you're as keen as when you're against it—which is something with many people. Do you follow that?

NR:

Yes, I do.

ES:
For instance, in the history of religion there have been people who go from skepticism to faith. However, they don't feel they're as keen when they have faith. When they're skeptical, they're keen. If you don't feel just as keen having faith, you might as well get out of the religion business, because you're only at a weak, submissive moment. Faith—the true thing—is just as sharp as any doubt. That is something to see, because most people think that when they care for Aesthetic Realism, somehow they're slipping. Like Mr. Carduner, he feels he's gone soft in some strange way.

NR:
Do I?

ES:
Yes. If you don't, we'd like to hear it. Just say "I love Aesthetic Realism, and I don't think I'm soft a bit." Whenever you love anything, you think you're jelly, Rosenthal.

KK:
That's right.

NR:
I love Aesthetic Realism, and I don't think I'm soft.

ES:
I don't believe it, Rosenthal. Do you want me to believe it?

NR:
No, I do feel softer, I guess.

ES:

That's something else—softer. We'll look into the meaning of that. But one of the things that everybody has to do is to put their hardness and softness together, to put the buzz saw and the petal together. You have that job.

DT:

Mr. Siegel, is going for despair a hardening of yourself?

ES:

It very often is, yes. It's not the hardening, it's a hardening of something. The relation between hardness and softness is exceedingly subtle. Let's say a person—I describe it very often—a person argues like hell, "I'll never give in. What are you trying to tell me! No, no, no!" And then he goes off to his room and starts crying. Do you see the hardness and the softness as two phases of one thing?

NR:

Yes.

ES:

When people are hard, it's because they're soft about something they don't want to look at. Anytime you're hard with another person wrongly, you're soft with your ego. People would rather be soft with their egos than hard. The relation— there's much to say on the subject. However, the problem still remains that when you're hard and when you're soft, you should have the same purpose. For instance, let's say I say to Rosenthal: "I appreciate very much, Norma Rosenthal, your interest in Aesthetic Realism and your constancy about it. I think it's lovely." I say that in a certain way. I also say that I think you want to deceive me into thinking you care more for it than you really do. Do you think I have the same motive in saying that?

NR:
Yes, I do.

ES:
All right, check. I said the first, and it's complimentary. That's what people don't want to believe—that I have the same motive. I wish people would ask. For example, when Mr. Kimmelman had his film here, I said very good things. Two weeks later I was unfaithful to him. The question is: what was the motive? Anyway—I don't think you care as much for Aesthetic Realism as sometimes you like to appear.

NR:
I think you're right. I'd like to see more about it.

ES:
Why can't you say it in a stronger way? Look, many people have distrusted other people, and then they find they trust me a little more than they do other people—they think they're soft. If they're soft, stop it! I don't want to be trusted by soft people! Do you understand? If this isn't as keen as anything, then stop it—we'll wait. (Applause) I've asked people again and again—you can do it tomorrow—talk about my motives all night; tell the damnedest, but don't think if you trust me, you're being soft. You're being sharp! If not, stop it! It's insulting and its very hurtful. That's why I said to Mr. Hansen, when he said something about my patronizing—everyone wants to feel that: they think if they care for Aesthetic Realism, they're soft. That's a goddamn lie! You didn't want to care for it, and you did everything you could not to, and if you did, it's because

some other sharpness came through! Stop pretending! Do you get what I'm talking about?

NR:
Yes.

ES:
Mr. Kimmelman liked to think that. He'll try to give that appearance whenever he can. When you care for something you want to give the appearance that you've softened. That should stop in you, Miss Rosenthal. (Reads note)

> "Mr. Siegel—about four weeks ago Norma became angry and went to a fortune teller. I have noticed that she has an interest in astrology and reacts seriously to it."

Yes? One thing that the Catholic church and I agree upon: we think that astrology is a waste of time for anything but the stars. The stars benefit, but nothing else does.

BS:
I don't even think they do.

NR:
I don't even know why I go there.

ES:
Now, now. Did you ever hear of the Law of Least Resistance?

NR:
No.

ES:
What people would like—every person would like to be as happy as possible with as little work as possible.

NR:
Yes.

ES:
Which do you think provides more work, astrology or Aesthetic Realism?

NR:
Aesthetic Realism.

ES:
Some people know that. Kestenbaum-Stern, do you think that Aesthetic Realism means some work?

Faith K.-Stern:
It sure does. I used to say it was much easier to go to a psychiatrist than study Aesthetic Realism.

ES:
Aren't you working now? If you aren't getting a workout now—

NR:
I am.

ES:
You are, definitely. You're working like anything.

NR:
I am.

ES:

I'm asking you to see things, and then see some other things, and then relate them. Something in you doesn't like that. Take that eminent workman, Mr. Carduner. Wouldn't you like to have it easier?

JC:

Yes.

ES:

Of course, you would. I think everybody here would. So it's just by chance you went to astrology?

NR:

(Laughs) No, I guess—

ES:

Do you believe you like my attitude to you?

NR:

Yes, I do like your attitude to me.

ES:

You shouldn't. I'm one of the coldest people that ever was.

NR:

No, you're not.

ES:

You know that.

NR:

But I don't feel it.

ES:
You don't feel it?

NR:
No. (Company disagrees)

FKS:
Mr. Siegel, I really feel I have to object. I feel that what you're saying today is the toughest thing going. I think when Miss Rosenthal is home alone, if she's anything like me, she doesn't give a soft soap job that she can give here now. I feel you know why you went to that astrologer. You wanted an easier answer.

ES:
Sure.

BB:
Also all week she was in pain and she was scared of you; she was scared of what you were going to tell her.

ES:
I take for granted, Miss Rosenthal, that you hate me; which I do with about everyone; meaning by that, there's a certain way of mind that isn't seen as tenderness or love. That goes for everyone. I think that that could be seen better. I think—I have to say this; it sounds gushy, but I think I'm accurate about love and am for it in a way the largeness of which hasn't been seen yet. I have to be careful, otherwise I'll sound gushy. It is not care or love as people want it right away. Do you think, for instance, you would like to have contempt for me?

NR:
I probably would.

ES:

Everybody would. They hate me because I don't give them the chance. When I do, I take it back—I hope so. One of the things I've said is that we cannot love anything we can't have contempt for; and if a person doesn't give us grounds for contempt, that is changed into not caring for us. It's an awful thing, but pain is a teacher. I've seen that unless people have contempt for me, they'll never, never think I care for them. What do you think of that?

NR:

I don't think that's true.

ES:

Everything I say can be talked about on a Monday. I think people are still looking for contempt, and they're angry with me because they haven't got it in the size they want. They think if I don't give it to them, I don't care for them. Say that as a cold proposition. People think that they're entitled to it. I believe people should discuss that where there's anything to discuss.

DT:

Mr. Siegel, I'm not wholly sure about what you mean.

ES:

I'll try to explain it. It will be talked of more. There are these two reasons. It's in the orange card. I imagine I'll be explaining this as long as I can explain anything. There are two reasons for thinking you're somebody: one, because you go around the world and you look at things and even the greatest shops and the biggest institutions have something false about them, and so you can have contempt. Every time you have contempt, it gets to be a little regimental stripe for yourself, a little medal. People, without knowing it, this is what they're nourished by: how many things in this world they can have contempt for. It keeps them going in a way. In a way—it's not a true way. The other way of feeling that every time you respect something, that is the time you respect yourself, is goddamn hard. I'm the only person who says it, and people have given me an awful time. They don't want to believe it. I still say it. It's a hard thing, and I have to say that the more people respect me, they respect themselves. If they don't run away, they'll see they do. They do run away. They find its too hard to bear. Mr. Kimmelman has done that. He finds that he respects me, and he thinks he's less. Now what Aesthetic Realism says is this: The way to respect yourself is honestly to respect as much in this world as possible. That is the only way. But the other way is mighty easy. Since people look for it and thrive by it, if they find that they can't have it—. There was a woman here, Regina Dienes—Regina Bogat—Louis Dienes's wife. She said that. She said "We're angry with you because we can't have contempt for you." I still remember that. And though we had disagreements, I'm thankful to her. I didn't have to say it myself. Do you remember that?

Martha Baird:
Oh yes, I remember.

ES:
There are some people who remember it. Persons will think I don't care for them because I don't give them the chance to get that contempt so easily. That's the one reason. That's why Aesthetic Realism has such a hard time and why many people didn't come yesterday, because they're looking for their contempt traffic, and they think they're entitled to it. They

have a notion they won't get so much by coming to Aesthetic Realism. Yes?

NR:
I was thinking about that.

ES:
You think about that. I say you want to have contempt for me. I say it about everybody.

David Bernstein:
Mr. Siegel, do people think it's part of having a good time having contempt?

ES:
They don't think about it. You see, when a child for instance eats, a child doesn't say, "I'm now getting nourishment and calories." Contempt goes that way. You have it. You don't have to say, "I go for it." You go for it. You will find a child getting a pleasure from contempt in early months.

ER:
I have something to support this. In my class last week we were talking about point three on the orange card.* One girl just said, "We do that all the time."

*Four statements of Aesthetic Realism: 1) Every person is always trying to put together opposites in himself. 2) Every person in order to respect himself has to see the world as beautiful or acceptable. 3) There is a disposition in every person to think he will be for himself by making less of the outside world. 4) All beauty is the making one of opposites, and the making one of opposites is what we are going after in ourselves.

ES:
Right. It is seen as the order of the day.

NR:
That's right.

ES:
Anyway, when I talk to people about themselves, they watch me like hawks: am I honest? You're watching me like a hawk now, Rosenthal. I don't mind that. Only be a good hawk. Don't mind if you don't find it. They watch me like hawks: when is this person going to show the bad motive and the phoniness I'm entitled to? I would like this to be discussed. Everybody thinks they're entitled to find me a phony. I don't think anyone has stopped yet. Do you think something in you wants to find me a phony?

NR:
Yes, because I do it in other people.

ES:
You hope to.

NR:
I do it with you, too.

ES:
Why shouldn't you?

NR:
I mean, I shouldn't do it. I know I do it.

ES:

Please. I'm trying to explain why you can feel bad. Let's say a person hopes to find me a phony and he feels "Goddamn it, I haven't." They get angry with me, they get depressed, and sometimes they want to die. That's one of the reasons Nat Herz wanted to die. He just thought he'd find me a phony.

NR:

(Unclear)

ES:

Yes. It's one of the reasons that his desire for life wasn't as strong. He just felt he was entitled to it. Like the woman we were talking about yesterday who Miss Reiss knows. She also felt she was entitled to it, Harriet Fitch, now Zinnes. This is there. People are entitled, and they get angry with me, because they don't see that respect is the real food. The fact that they cannot go for that makes them angry, and they think either I'm unkind, or I'm such a good fooling mechanism that I can fool people where before they weren't so fooled. It couldn't be that I feel that maybe honesty is a good thing.

Anyway, this is what I say: I hope that while you're honest, you respect me as much as possible. If it's ten times more than today, it's okay. It will be keen and factual; as much as the honest traffic can bear. Do you understand? I hope you don't go through that junk that people have: "My God, I have to see something phony. I have to do some disrespecting. Why can't I get something on him that sticks?"

NR:

Thank you.

ES:
If you talk with people, if they talked honestly, they'd say yes, everybody's tried to get my number.

MB:
Everybody has.

ES:
Everybody has. They're just watching for the real slip-up.

MB:
I feel right now people are angry because—

ES:
Let them be angry. The hell with them! Is that clear?

Jack Musicant:
I respect what you're saying. I haven't found anything in twenty-three years, and I really feel good about that.

ES:
I hope so. You can feel good. I think the purpose of every unconscious is to respect something honestly. Otherwise, you gyp yourself. If I provide a chance for respect, I am meeting your deepest hopes. I hope you don't louse it up. I say again and again: To hell with the contempt principle in you. While it works in anybody, the hell with it! (Applause) Everybody here is troubled by their feeling that they may be a hypocrite. So Miss Rosenthal, since this lesson is tough, have you been troubled by that?

NR:
Yes, Mr. Siegel.

ES:
Why do you say it sadly?

NR:
I should be happy.

ES:
It's this: you have to ask why I asked it. Is it in order to have you feel bad?

NR:
No.

ES:
It happens that this is the trouble: people feel they're two people and if they're two people, one must be lying.

NR:
Yes. Mr. Siegel, I want to tell you sincerely. Yesterday I thought about it. I thought about one example where I could be doing it. I asked myself whether, when you praised Margot Carpenter, were you as sincere as when you praised me or when you give a criticism?

ES:
All right, keep on asking.

NR:
Or when you praise somebody else?

ES:
I haven't called Miss Carpenter the greatest master of the sonnet. I'm thinking of doing it, though.

MC:
I'll live for the day!

NR:
That makes me feel more sure.

ES:
I'm trying to understand you. What was it you were saying?

NR:
I felt—I asked myself whether I thought it was sincere when you praised Margot as when you praised me.

ES:
Let's be specific. Praise is a general term. What did I praise Miss Carpenter for? In one way or another, I praised nearly everybody here. I praised Mr. Carduner for a communication lately.

NR:
I used her as an example. But when you do give praise—

ES:
What did I praise her for?

DT:
Mr. Siegel, she said it wrong in the first place. You said that Miss Carpenter was a better critic.

ES:
Was a better critic?

DT:
Yes, of people.

ES:

Well, Miss Carpenter is a better critic of people. Once she was looking for admiration, and when you look for admiration too intently, it interferes with your critical powers. Yes, I've said this to others. I'll say that Irene Reiss is a better critic; Kestenbaum-Stern is a better critic.

BB:

I said the same thing yesterday, and she spoke about it last night.

ES:

Let's be clear. The purpose of Aesthetic Realism is to encourage you to be a better critic of yourself and of people. Mr. Musicant is a better critic. I try to have Mr. Bonura a better critic of himself and other people. At certain times, in the field of poetry, I feel—and others said it—about the Cummings paper. In various ways I think that Miss Carpenter is seeing people better. Mrs. Mondlin is seeing people better. Aren't you?

Miriam Mondlin:

I certainly am.

NR:

This is what—I should see more why I feel this way, but it's not—

ES:

Look, make a statement. If you want to take a statement, for instance, that I praise people—that doesn't mean very much. I praised Mr. Krakauer. I try to be specific. I don't give what can be called an all-out encomium. Yes?

ERASING SCARS

BB:
I think what she wants—

ES:
I praised you.

BB:
Yes. When you praised Margot, I took the praise to myself too yesterday. What she wants to say, which I think is not clear, is that when you said that praise yesterday, she didn't think it was sincere. That's what she should say.

ES:
That's right.

NR:
That's what I wanted to say.

ES:
Will you say it; then?

NR:
I asked myself—

ES:
Look, Miss Carpenter once had a book of poems here, and I was quite fierce with it. I tried to be kind. I said it's the wrong approach—really, it came to that—it's the wrong approach to poetry. I also, when I have talked to her, I've told her that there was this desire to have a man at her feet and accept her instantaneously and for eternity. I must say I'm proud of the fact that Miss Carpenter has listened. She may want to stop listening. That is something to consider. But what was it that I said that you felt was insincere?

NR:

I didn't feel that—I just asked myself whether I thought that that was just as sincere as when you were talking to me. I mean, that's the only reason when you asked me—

ES:

Will you get to specific statements? As far as I know, I try to be sincere with everyone. For instance, I'm proud of Mr. Spears that he hasn't run away. Next week, we're going to have a praise of Mrs. D'Amico in the D'Amico lesson. I remember Miss Davis wrote a communication lately, and she was praised for that. Miss Davis, have I ever praised you?

Joan Davis:

Yes, you have, Mr. Siegel.

ES:

You see, there's a contest between you and Miss Carpenter, unfortunately. (Company agrees) I got into it. I don't think you girls are the best friends yet.

NR:

No, we're not.

ES:

Whom do you like more, your brother or Miss Carpenter?

NR:

Miss Carpenter.

ES:

You do?

NR:
Yes.

ES:
So, what do you dislike about your brother?

NR:
He's insincere.

ES:
That's all? No. He makes you less.

NR:
He makes me less.

ES:
A brother very often does that to a sister.

NR:
That's right, he does.

ES:
He makes you less. The good fortune of Miss Singer is she never had one of those brothers. However, she had a sister to make her less with.

BS:
Yes.

ES:
But a brother can do it fine. Mr. Bonura has a brother who makes him less; he hates him like anything. Don't you?

Aldo Bonura:
Hmmm.

ES:
Do you remember that brother?

AB:
Yes, I do.

ES:
You remember. I'm sorry to say I do. (Laughter)

MB:
He can't say he hates anybody.

Carmen de Gomar:
I don't know, I don't know whether to dare say the things that Miss Rosenthal has said publicly about her brother. She said he's dirty, he's a pig, he's a slob, he's sloppy.

NR:
When did I say that?

CdG:
Your brother. When? (Laughter)

ES:
This was in the dream.

CdG:
Nobody can live with him.

NR:
When did I say that?

ES:
Miss Rosenthal had a dream about this brother.

CdG:
When? I don't know—I don't remember the date exactly.

ES:
You have seen your brother as a critic of you. In this dream your brother is a critic. That is a very big thing, because it means that your contempt had a field day with him. He is saying to you, "Though you've criticized me, I also have a right to criticize you"—in this dream. Do you follow that? How do you feel?

NR:
I feel–

ES:
Mr. Kimmelman, what do you think? I'm trying to be useful to Miss Rosenthal.

KK:
As to how she feels?

ES:
Yes.

KK:
I feel that she's stunned.

ES:
Stunned? You at least had a little preparation. Now Miss Rosenthal, would you be specific? You still haven't said what you've heard that you feel was insincere. If it's insincere, then it's my fault, and you should not like it. But what was it that you felt was insincere?

NR:

What I can make up in my mind to be insincere.

ES:

There may be something. It happens a good deal. Sometimes people think I'm praising somebody all over the place. Often sometimes there is a person. Let's say Mr. Kimmelman. He was getting a great deal of praise when he presented this film. At one time Miss Le Monds got a great deal of praise. Do you remember that? I think Mr. Bonura also—

AB:

That's right.

ES:

I know I praised Mr. Musicant only recently.

BB:

Mr. Siegel, when I used to live with Faith Stern, I used to get very angry every time you used to praise her, because I felt you used to make less of me, instead of seeing more exact. I think that's what she feels, and she doesn't want to express it.

ES:

As soon as I use the praise of one person against another, then I should be told that.

ER:

I feel that—

ES:

I praised you.

ER:
Yes. I feel that there's more known about this than is said. I feel that every person wants to be the one praised most. It's one of the things used to feel you're cold and not caring. I feel that Norma—because I have done this—feels anyone who gets praise at a time when she doesn't, is getting praised insincerely. Then she can feel when she's praised, it's insincere.

ES:
What do you think of Miss Carpenter? Do you think she's honest? You can say it. After all, Miss Carpenter has gone through so much already—you can go through this.

MC:
I can take it.

ES:
Yes. What do you think?

NR:
I think she's honest. As to me and the way she sees me, I don't think she's honest with me.

ES:
There was one time I was saying to Miss Carpenter—there was a friend she had, Mr. Stanton, I believe—

MC:
Stoddard.

ES:
Stoddard. Sorry. I knew it began with S-t. I said to Miss Carpenter at that time, that she used Mr. Stoddard against

Aesthetic Realism. There was thought of coming to the Terrain Gallery at that time, and I was quite intense. In fact, I talked about Mr. Stoddard somewhat the way I could about your brother or somebody like that. Here is the thing: Do you feel I want to see what is good in you and say it's there?

NR:
Yes, I do.

ES:
Some people think I don't praise anybody. I do praise, and my purpose is to encourage other people, not to get them down! That's an insult! I never praised a person in order to get anybody else down. I wish people would stop it!

NR:
I hope to stop it.

ES:
This is the thing: there are many persons who feel that you cannot love Aesthetic Realism and still have yourself. Miss Carpenter has that problem. Can she care for Aesthetic Realism, can she respect me and still be a living person in her own right? What do you think?

NR:
I think so, yes.

ES:
You don't think so! Because every time I praised a person it was to encourage. I remember Mr. Herz used to get very mad because I praised people, and he didn't want to see that the reason I praised them, was to show that somebody could care

for Aesthetic Realism and still look good to himself and to herself.

Nancy Starrels:
Mr. Siegel, I'd like to say something about this. First of all, I would like to say that I think that you've been as critical of Margot Carpenter as practically I've heard you be of anybody. That happens to be so. But the—more important than that, I feel that this, which everybody has done—this thing about who you're praising and who you're not—everyone has done it. God knows I have. I feel—

ES:
Remember, it was felt that I was praising Barbara Lekberg all over the place, and somehow the lady left.

NS:
Quite true. I feel it's one of the ways of whittling away and showing ones anger with the respect we have for you. Otherwise, I don't think it would happen.

ES:
It should be gone into. This is the important thing: I don't have a right to use one person against another. And if I should praise someone in such a way that it would make and should make other people feel less hope in themselves, that would be a bad thing to do. Wherever that was done, I rescind it if I can. But when—I think everyone knows that Margot Carpenter has had difficulty in sticking with Aesthetic Realism. Do you think so?

NR:
(Nods yes)

MB:
She doesn't think so. (Company agrees)

ES:
Well, she has. There are other people who have had difficulty. Mr. Perey has had difficulty. The person who is going to have the next lesson, Miss Musicant, has had difficulty. I have to think of that. I feel that if people don't run away, they can make sense out of Aesthetic Realism and me. The only thing is that they want to get angry, which is another form of running away. So do you think I'm using Margot Carpenter now to have you have less hope or more hope?

NR:
More hope.

ES:
I hope you believe that. Do you?

NR:
Yes I do. I do believe it.

ES:
I hope you do.

NR:
I want to believe it more.

ES:
I don't think you believed it in the past, anyway.

NR:
In the past?

ES:

In the past—up until the moment you said you did believe it.

NR:

It's going to change. I want it to.

ES:

If it's changed, good. Let's applaud. I'm not sure, but let's applaud anyway. (Applause from company) Look, at one time, Mrs. Musicant and Mr. Musicant would be here, and both of them felt I was using one against the other, and both wanted to leave sometimes. I can mention other people. I can say this: If I did that, I should stop having lessons because everything would get into a mess. Do you think I see you as you?

NR:

Yes.

ES:

All right. You have had two kinds of praise: one, men and relatives have given it to you as they gave Miss de Gomar. She once had an album here of all the people who have praised her. (Laughter) And also you got a great deal of praise through what contempt you found. Every time we find contempt, it's an indirect praise of ourselves. You want to study Aesthetic Realism. Do you think I made any mistake about you? I'll listen if you think so.

NR:

No, Mr. Siegel.

ES:

All right. But do you believe there are things in you that seem that way?

NR:
I haven't seen—

ES:
I have this responsibility: To have every person's life, encourage every person's life, to be as good as it can be. I try to stick to that.

NR:
You do, Mr. Siegel.

ES:
What was, then, the criticism that you had?

NR:
Contempt.

ES:
No, no. You said something. People have criticized me—they don't fool me. Everybody has been critical. I just wish they'd be more specific. I'm proud of Mr. Hansen; he said he felt I patronized him. At least it was something specific. Just what? Miss Kestenbaum-Stern felt I was critical of her in a way I wasn't with other people sometimes. So where?

NR:
I'm trying to think.

ES:
What people have to do is to make a useful comparison between talk in social life and talk here. There is a relation. The important thing is: I promise everybody I'll never appeal to the weakness in them. I might do it without knowing it; but that is what goes on in social life: people appeal to the

weakness in order to be popular. If anybody ever felt I appealed to the weakness, please object. Persons want their weakness to be appealed to because it's very pleasing. Do you know what I mean? I have tried not to appeal to the weakness. I have tried not to appeal to the weakness of Mr. Krakauer. Would you like me to appeal to your weakness a little?

GK:
Somewhere I would, yes.

ES:
Of course you would—it's fun. Yes?

NR:
Yes.

ES:
So let's know what's going on. The way I see it, people weaken each other in social life. They have this inter-contempt team, this inter-flattery team; they don't know they're using it. Even while they're weakened by it, people still yearn for it and hate me for not giving it.

MB:
I have a question. How did your praise of Margot Carpenter and encouragement of her yesterday, even assuming it was incorrect, how did it hurt Norma Rosenthal?

ES:
Yes, that's a good question. How? She could have less trust in me—in that way it could be. Yes?

NR:

I felt it wasn't fair for me to be thinking that way. I felt that it was not logical.

ES:

Do you believe people are competitive?

NR:

Yes, I do.

ES:

Do you think it makes for trouble?

NR:

Yes.

ES:

Of course, they are. Then they make me as one of the persons in the competition.

KK:

Can you say how you've become involved in the competition?

ES:

Instead of seeing my purpose, I'm seen socially: I prefer one person to another. The use of the word prefer—for instance, I'll say very definitely—I have certain opinions. There was a girl here, Miss Waterhouse. I felt that she might leave. I have those opinions. I feel some people don't like Aesthetic Realism as much as other people do. But the question is: On what basis do I think that? If I see a person wanting to do something—for instance, take the person who was here, Mr. Feldmesser. I was quite aware; I tried to be as gentle and kind. I know certain things never appealed to him. I want to be careful. I knew that his care for Aesthetic Realism, there was something not complete about it. That goes for everybody. I'm a critic. I don't like people who play politics with Aesthetic Realism. I'll be fair to them, but I don't like it! Do you understand?

NR:
Yes.

ES:
If I say to a person: Look, Ellen Reiss, you care more for Aesthetic Realism now than some other persons—the reason is to help Aesthetic Realism. It's true. Why shouldn't I use it? The question is: am I trying to be unfair? For instance, Barbara Allen showed a great care for Aesthetic Realism. I acknowledged it. I think she's had some difficult times. Things can happen. I think I tried to acknowledge your interest. The thing is, I do judge people's honesty, how much they honestly love Aesthetic Realism. If you want to hold that against me, go ahead.

NR:
No.

ES:
That's the way I judge it. I do see people playing politics. I'll do the best I can. I give all the energy I can in the lesson. But at the same time, I cannot say I like it. If you want me to trust you entirely, Miss Rosenthal, you can ask for it and show me where I could more—I'd be glad to. But I feel that there is this desire to be pained by Aesthetic Realism with all the good things you say. I could say this of other people. For instance, Mrs. Mellon. I have said to her very often—as she talks to a

friend of hers in the same apartment, I convey my distrust. Have I?

Anna Mellon:
Yes, you have.

ES:
What was the purpose? To make you feel bad? I've made it very clear. I think America should love Aesthetic Realism. The people here are the persons who in a human way have been entrusted with that purpose, because they have met it first-hand. If they want to go and act selfish, as some people have, they don't want to say something—the dream of Mr. Stern yesterday where he felt bad because he didn't say what he had to. I think everybody who doesn't want Aesthetic Realism to be known feels like a heel and feels awful. Also, anybody who wants to cheapen it or not respect me. If you want to deny that, you can deny it. I have some notion of the persons who would like to cheapen and the persons who don't want to cheapen so much. Yes, Miss Rosenthal?

NR:
How do I stand? (Company objects to question)

ES:
Miss Rosenthal, you see, that's completely irrelevant. Either you ask ... This is the question that you and Miss Carpenter have and Miss Singer has—there's only one question: Did I try to do the best for your life as I saw it?

NR:
Yes, you have.

ES:

All right. Then be happy. You're here. There's a lesson. Once there is a lesson, I do the best I can. You have the same question as Mr. Carduner: What is my motive? Have I tried to do the best for his life or not? Mr. Bonura. Do you understand? I try to present that which I think a person is looking for and which in a way his life needs. I tried to do that today. I thought of talking much more about your brother, I must say, also your sister. I think it's important. But the lesson—I sometimes can control a lesson, and sometimes I can't. The lesson has gone this way, so I think that is the best. When you say "Where do I stand?" to me that's an irrelevant question. The question is: in talking to you will I do the best? You could ask Mr. Dienes, does he think I do the best when I talk to him? Mr. Dienes?

Louis Dienes:

I think you do, Mr. Siegel.

ES:

We've had many arguments. I don't like the way Louis Dienes sees Aesthetic Realism. He's seen it clearly. I feel he and his father are still in a cheapening team. Have I made that clear?

LD:

Yes, you have.

ES:

And you haven't had too much energy to get out of it. You've suffered a great deal. Have I made that clear?

NR:

That's right. I don't feel that I like the way I see Aesthetic Realism wholly, either.

ES:

All right. I said something like that a long time ago to Louis Dienes. So what's the kick? It's a matter of having the best way of seeing win, or the best thought win. If people's way of seeing Aesthetic Realism is the best for them, let it win. Yes?

MB:

I have watched you as a critic of people for a great many years. One of the things I've observed is that you don't at any one time say everything. For one thing, you couldn't. Very often you surprised me both by a kind of praise or encouragement of a person where I thought they were up to something; or sometimes a severity where I thought, oh, you know, they're really doing very good, why do you see it that way? My consensus is that you judge the situation and the person in terms of what does that person need most at this moment, to bring out his strength. Sometimes, though, a person is doing very well apparently, there will be a touch of something complacent, and you know it's the worst thing possible for that person, and you will be very severe at a sign of it.

ES:

Still, it comes down to this: Am I doing the best I can see for a person?

MB:

Yes.

ES:

I want to say again—what is the question?

MB:

Are you doing the best for a person?

ES:
People see that. Don't misquote me. Once I'm not doing the best I can see for a person, please object. I cannot see something. Occasionally a whole lesson changes because I get a note.

MB:
Right, sometimes you don't have information.

ES:
Yes.

Albert Mondlin:
I believe that, Mr. Siegel, you are fair as much as what you see, and I believe that your desire to see is more complete than I have seen in anyone else. I wanted to say a very important thing which I'm not sure everyone heard. When you asked Miss Rosenthal what she thought of Margot Carpenter, she said that Margot was honest. Then she said very quietly that Margot wasn't honest to her. I feel she could change that into saying, if you praise Miss Carpenter and you don't know all the facts—

ES:
I'm sure I don't. I'm sure I don't.

AM:
I feel that's like a jewel that a person can hold on to in a very bad way.

ES:
People can substitute one thing for another in a way that's inaccurate.

BS:

I've suffered as much as anybody, Mr. Siegel, when you praised other people. It finally came to me that there's something for me to learn every time you praise another person than myself. Ever since I saw that, I've been happier.

ES:

Good. Now, for instance, a matter has come to me: Mr. Perey's thesis. Now listen, Rosenthal. I do not trust Mr. Perey on the subject of Aesthetic Realism entirely. I never gave that feeling. I've praised him. I know he's done various things, including financial things, but also he was disappointed by a book he was working on with Vana Earle and Mr. Bonura. He would like to get the favor of Columbia and the people there. However, it is very important also that Aesthetic Realism be presented in the best way. There now is a committee headed by Martha Baird which is called the Look At Committee. When any publication is in process that will reach other people, Miss Baird is entitled to look at it and ask two other people or so to look at it to make sure that it's just to Aesthetic Realism. Do you follow that, Mr. Perey?

Arnold Perey:

Yes.

ES:

I'm putting on the dog there because I don't trust people on this subject. Occasionally, it gets so effusive that it makes Aesthetic Realism look like revelation in a bad way. Then they get disappointed, and something else occurs. The best thing at this time is to have people concerned about it, so that when Aesthetic Realism is expressed elsewhere, it is in the truest fashion. So this committee, the Look At Committee exists.

Where this is related is: Do you think I should trust you when you talk about Aesthetic Realism to some people?

NR:
No.

ES:
Why? Just as I said to Mr. Perey. I think he's been hurt by me. I've hurt him, too, haven't I?

AP:
I think so.

ES:
You're not the only person I've hurt, if that's any consolation. I hurt Mr. Bonura.

NR:
I guess I tend to be pushy when I talk, and I also get angry fast. I get irritated.

ES:
Yes, of course. We were talking about that. We have to see why you get irritated. There's a reason. If you get irritated too fast, the desire is a little ahead of the facts. It would follow mathematically from that.

NR:
I don't understand.

ES:
It would mean there are two reasons why we get irritated: One is the facts that we have before us, and the other a hope that is in everybody to be irritated. They should coincide, like two

instruments in a duet. But sometimes the desire goes ahead of the facts. How do you feel now?

NR:
I feel good.

ES:
Yes? (Company disagrees)

NR:
I feel—

ES:
I remember when Miss Van Outryve was having her first lesson. I worried about her. Miss Van Outryve was suggested, I think, by Miss Carpenter.

NR:
I feel that I heard what I want to hear. I want to hear more. (Company disagrees)

JC:
I think Norma Rosenthal—the conceited self in her would be irritated, staggered and hurt now. It all wasn't just wonderful.

NR:
Yes.

ES:
Why don't you say, Miss Carpenter: "I didn't find it that easy, Miss Rosenthal." You can say it.

MC:
I would like to very much. I didn't find it that easy, Miss Rosenthal.

ES:
I asked her to say it. It's my fault.

MC:
Mr. Siegel, I have a question. Since this competition was first mentioned, it concerned me quite a bit. In a way I was surprised when it was first mentioned. I was wondering if there is something that I did particularly or that I could do that I don't do that would be more useful.

ES:
You give forth a certain confidence in yourself. You may not feel it. It annoys people for various reasons. You affect people like the image of Queen Elizabeth and so on. Persons, a girl, can feel you're too pleased with yourself. Then you may be suffering like anything, but they feel that your road is made up of flattery, more flattery to be, daisies and roses and Margot Carpenter.

It annoys people. Yes, Miss Rosenthal?

NR:
Yes, you can feel—I felt—

ES:
You see, when Miss Rosenthal is worried, as now, there's a very sad look in her eye. It happens that people hit each other the wrong way. You can seem too pleased with yourself, too confident in yourself, Miss Carpenter. There are many other things to say.

MC:
Thank you very much.

BB:
I'd like to make Margot Carpenter feel better. You aren't the only one that she has against.

MC:
I didn't think I was. I know how I feel about other women, so I know how someone else—something of how someone else feels.

ES:
The thing is, it's hard to use another person for our best interest in life. You can be used, as others can. I could mention a great deal of that. For instance, sometimes Miss Mellon seems so well groomed to people that they're envious of her and say things against her. Has that happened?

AM:
I think so.

ES:
The motto is: Don't be well groomed. Anyway, do you feel that the good that you met is greater than all this confusion?

NR:
Yes.

ES:
Do you think I used Miss Carpenter against you?

NR:
I don't feel it now.

ES:
I hope you don't, but you have felt it.

NR:
I have felt it.

MB:
She said she didn't feel it now.

ES:
You have felt it.

NR:
I have felt it in the past.

MB:
She has and might again.

NR:
I hope not.

ES:
I want to tell you this: I never saw yet the paper on Cummings that Miss Carpenter wrote. It was praised by Martha Baird and some others. Does that mean anything to you?

NR:
Yes, it does mean something to me.

ES:
Still, I have this—it may be careless, but I think that when Martha Baird praises a paper on poetry and some other people do—you saw it too?

ER:
Yes, I did.

ES:
I ask sometimes when I should participate and when not. It happens that the reason that the Poetry Group stopped taking up poems was because people made too much of my favorable criticism and too much of my unfavorable. That's not the only reason. I have a difficult time myself because I know I don't want to praise anybody to make anybody else less. That I know. But one can fumble. So the question is: Has that been?

NR:
It hasn't been. I know it hasn't.

ES:
I would like Aesthetic Realism to be associated with the good of this world; whatever is good in this world be associated with Aesthetic Realism, including, if need be, wealth where rightly used. Sports, I don't mind. Yachts even, I don't mind. I'd like Aesthetic Realism to be seen as a oneness of criticism and also hope and charm.

JM:
I want to applaud that statement: I would like Aesthetic Realism to be associated with the good of this world. (Applause from company)

ES:
Miss Brody, what do you care to say?

Ellen Brody:
I feel that I've heard criticism similar to this and had feelings similar to those of Miss Rosenthal. I can say pretty carefully

after being very cynical and not having a very good hope, that you do want to see the good in a person and say it.

ES:
I want to encourage what is best in their lives. That sounded a little sentimental.

EB:
You do want to encourage a person to be as good as they can be and see what they have against themselves.

ES:
I want to be judged in this way: I try to bring out the best in a person. If I don't do that, people should object. I may not see that right away, but as I see it I try to have it stronger in a person. That is the personal motive. The other is to present the world as well as I honestly can.

BB:
Mr. Siegel, I'd like to say from what I have seen. You did bring the best possibility of a person. That thing in itself is what made the change of every student's life.

ES:
That's the way I'd like to be judged. Have I tried to bring out the best? Once you try to bring out the best, there is good will. Then if you have some other motive, it doesn't go along with that. Yes?

MB:
I thought from the very moment that this lesson began, and after Norma Rosenthal wrote the document and said she felt she's at her first Communion, you started to ask about her ugly thoughts—your purpose was to bring together the two parts of

herself so that where she's angelic and she can be, and where she curses everything and hurts herself and things, they not be so far apart.

ES:
Yes.

MB:
That was what was gone after. Something in us wants that more than anything. Also, something wants to keep those things apart and doesn't like them being brought together. I'm rooting for that in Norma Rosenthal that wants them together.

NR:
Thank you.

ES:
I have this from Miss de Gomar. I think our Spanish-speaking contingent doesn't get along too well. Do you want to hear this? Have you suffered enough?

NR:
I don't get along too well.

MB:
I hesitated about sending it, but I thought it brings in a new thing that might be good.

ES:
It's from Carmen de Gomar. (Reads note)

> "Everyone has commented to me on my translations. The only one who hasn't said anything is Norma. It would be valuable, as

she knows the language, to know what she thought."

NR:
I thought I said last night that I liked it. Didn't I, Berthe?

ES:
We all misjudge you. How many things do you want me to take back now? You (CdG) take back what you said. She did say it. Everybody heard her. We all heard you say that you liked Miss de Gomars translations. (To CdG) We don't want any more of your malice—do you hear that? (Laughter) Same as Carpenter.

NR:
I like them. I do. Congratulations. I do like them.

ES:
Do you want me to take anything back? You do sound better.

NR:
I'm happier than I seem to be. (Laughter) I know I am.

ES:
I hope that's so.

MB:
I hope this comforts Miss Rosenthal. I remember very distinctly a Sunday. Margot Carpenter was in the other room. She was crying. She wanted to leave so bad. She couldn't stand the things you had said to her. She didn't want to stay for the next lesson. People put their arms around her and begged her.

ES:

She's nothing but a dammed Protestant somewhere, that Carpenter. (Laughter)

MB:

And her eyes were full of tears, and she wanted to leave. Do you remember that, Margot? She was so humiliated; nobody ever talked to her that way in her whole life in front of everybody. I think she was persuaded, and she didn't leave. And then she felt better.

ES:

Yes, Miss Carpenter.

MC:

(With large emotion) That's true, and a week later I wrote my first poem. I thank you for the criticism of that day. It was the toughest I had ever heard.

ES:

Good. As I said, with Harriet Fitch when she was interested in that book—I felt that some of the things that I said to her didn't seem so cruel now. Anyway, we have the following. Do you think this should go on?

NR:

Yes.

ES:

Yes? I don't know.

BB:

I don't think so.

NR:
I think it should go on. It's all right.

ER:
I don't know whether this is in order. I'm very much affected by this lesson. I agree with what Martha Baird said about the two parts of Norma Rosenthal. It happens that I've been very affected by Norma Rosenthal and those two things in her. I feel there's a certain relation now between Margot Carpenter and Norma Rosenthal. I feel very moved because I feel I'm affected by the way sweetness and toughness are in Miss Carpenter and also in Miss Rosenthal. I think the relation of the two opposites both of them are hoping for—you are making possible in both of them. I wanted to say that. Maybe at this time, I could thank Miss Rosenthal for having a good effect on my life. I hope that she'll take this opportunity to care more for Aesthetic Realism.

NR:
Thank you.

ES:
Blessed is the peacemaker. This note—since Miss Rosenthal doesn't object:

> "Mr. Siegel—She has said many times she does not want to be associated with Spanish-speaking people. Berthe Bania"

NR:
That's true.

ES:

What should I say about it? I envy you. I wish I knew Spanish. I wish I could talk Spanish. I've tried to read a little of Don— every time I mispronounce it—

CdG:

Quixote.

ES:

Quixote—in the Spanish. I did a little. There are other things, too. In the meantime, will you reconsider?

NR:

Yes. I'm reconsidering.

ES:

What I would say is this: In order to reconsider, I ask Miss de Gomar and also Miss Reiss to try to put some of the things in this lesson into Spanish for you and see whether—since you say you like the lesson—once it takes the form of this language in debate now, how you see it.

CdG:

That's wonderful! (Company agrees)

ES:

You take three statements and Miss de Gomar takes three statements—and then if you (NR) want to take three statements, it's all right, too.

NR:

Okay.

ERASING SCARS

ES:
So you're all right?

NR:
Yes.

ES:
All right.

(Applause)

CONTEMPT CAUSES INSANITY:
by Eli Siegel

Reprinted from The Right of Aesthetic Realism to Be Known
Number 195, Dec, 22, 1976.

Dear Unknown Friends:

It is hard for the press to realize that Aesthetic Realism is a study in the fullest sense of the word. Relevant here is one of the definitions of study to be found in *The Pocket Oxford Dictionary* (1924): "devote time and thought to understanding (subject, facts, etc.)." This is the definition of study as a verb, and the noun continues the verb, settles it.

Anyway, to "devote time and thought to understanding" is just what the press has been unwilling to do. In these last days, the Aesthetic Realism Foundation has received some letters from personnel of the press asking rather splenetically and peremptorily: "What is Aesthetic Realism?" How I wish, dear unknown friends, the press truly wanted to know!

I am afraid, however, that the press wants to know as much as would give it a reason not to study. The press wants to "get" something on Aesthetic Realism; wants to be "disillusioned" and to cause disillusionment in others. The press in its unfriendliness, in its haste, in its engulfing snobbishness, has hurt its members and its members' relatives.

It is certainly hard for the press to see those persons who have studied Aesthetic Realism and found it true, as careful, analytic, observant people. The tendency on the part of the press is to see the persons who at close range and for some time have observed and evaluated Aesthetic Realism and found it true empirically and conceptually, as, for some reason, more gullible, more unwisely receptive than persons of the press are.

It wasn't true ten years ago and it isn't true now. When someone has found Aesthetic Realism to be true, it was first after having given Aesthetic Realism a severe and prolonged workout. The acceptance of Aesthetic Realism—and there is such a thing—is a culmination of some of the most doubting, diminishing mental procedures there ever were.

However, I feel it is right in this number of TRO to answer this question, too often asked peremptorily: What is Aesthetic Realism? I hope the press considers this answer.

1. A Study in Three Divisions

I have thought a good deal of how to present Aesthetic Realism succinctly, without depriving it of its comprehensiveness and richness. I have found it useful to see Aesthetic Realism as having three divisions. These divisions may, with one word or expression for each, be termed: I. Contempt; II. Opposites; III. Good Will.

The first division of Aesthetic Realism is, in relation to the life of now, the most immediate. Ah, if people knew that there was in them a desire for contempt of the world, all that is not themselves. Persons studying Aesthetic Realism have come to see this with meaning for them hourly and daily. William Atherton, noted American actor, a few days ago wrote to me from Los Angeles. He said:

> From you and Aesthetic Realism I have learned that an honest fight between respect and contempt is the greatest drama. It has the life of the world in it.

Mr. Athertons letter is of December 8, 1976. Long before 1976, contempt as a means of expressing strong, autonomous individuality was popular: with hurt ensuing.

My present attempt to show that contempt is the crucial or central cause of insanity began on October 15, 1975, with TRO 133. It is a pity, to use the word of last week, that my statement, Contempt Weakens Mind, and later, Contempt Causes Insanity, was not looked into by the psychiatric profession and by the press. The students of Aesthetic Realism, as the days went on, saw more reason or foundation in the seeing of self-elevating contempt as the cause of insanity. They are studying the matter; and that is right. If only the press saw Aesthetic Realism as requiring honest, steady attention, how much better things would be!

Those who care to consult TRO 133 and following numbers will find evidence coming from various aspects of reality for the statement: Contempt Causes Insanity. The evidence for this statement is to be found in many more places than I gave last year. As an instance, let us take the following, on page 124 of *Modern Clinical Psychiatry* by Noyes and Kolb (Fifth Edition, Philadelphia: Saunders, 1961):

A common form of compulsion is that of hand-washing.

The phrase, "I wash my hands of it," has been used in England and America for hundreds of years as a way of saying that a person wanted to get rid of something or give it as little meaning as possible. Certainly, then, compulsive washing of hands is concerned with contempt. We should like to wash our hands of all reality which has the temerity of not suiting us. Much literature exists in the psychiatric world on the subject of compulsive hand-washing. Is it not time, then, dear unknown friends, to see whether this compulsive hand-washing is a way of evincing contempt? And this way of evincing contempt is accompanied by so many others. I mentioned some of the ways in TRO 133 and later numbers.

And a young psychiatrist has accused his elders in the profession of having contempt for their patients and others. Robert Coles wrote an article, "A Young Psychiatrist Looks at His Profession," appearing in the *Atlantic Monthly,* July 1961. Dr. Coles writes:

> Most of us can recall our moments of arrogance, only thinly disguised by words which daily become more like shibboleths, sound hollow, and are almost cant .... When the heart dies, we slip into words and doctrinaire caricatures of life .... As the words grow longer and the concepts more intricate and tedious, human sorrows and temptations disappear, loves move away, envies and jealousies, revenge and terror dissolve .... We try to hide behind our couches, hide ourselves from our patients.

If, then, psychiatrists themselves can have contempt, it is likely quite popular with humanity as such. But I am writing about contempt now, not for the purpose of showing its extent and the harm it does, but to present the First Division of the answer to the question: What is Aethetic Realism?

I. Aesthetic Realism, seeing contempt as the main cause of mental weakness and of insanity, studies contempt as something everyone is disposed to have as a means of strengthening himself and of lessening the meaning of reality for himself.

2. *The Oppostites Are the Way*

How can a person like the world without deceiving oneself, without making the world nicer or more agreeable than it is? Aesthetic Realism sees aesthetics as the one means of liking the world that is not self-deceptive; or because one is so fortunately placed that liking the world comes easier than with those less fortunate.

In the same way as a nocturne of Chopin may be liked, with all its sadness, because some accurate, deep form accompanies the sad tonal message, the unwelcome can be so well seen it becomes a cause of strength for the person doing the seeing. The relation of good and evil in the world, of pleasure and pain, of the disappointing and enhancing, of life and death, Aesthetic Realism sees as an aesthetic relation. Good and Evil, so central in the everyday lives of all, are two opposites like line and color in painting, surface and depth in poetry, continuity and discontinuity in music, order and freedom in drama, oneness and manyness in architecture, sameness and change in the novel, harmony and surprise in the film.

Aesthetic Realism studies the opposites in all the arts as a means for an individual to see himself as containing rest and motion, say, the way a symphony does. The opposites comprise the Second Division of the study of Aesthetic Realism. This Second Division can, on this occasion, be expressed in the following manner:

II. Aesthetic Realism sees the world as the oneness of opposites, or aesthetics; and sees the oneness of opposites in the world as the one way of mitigating, lessening, and perhaps defeating the deep desire for contempt in everyone, with its accompanying mental weakening.

3. Good Will: Encouragement and Criticism

Aesthetic Realism sees good will as the aesthetic oneness of encouragement and criticism. If we are to be true to a friend, or anyone, we must hope to be able to tell him what he may be doing against himself. Criticism, Aesthetic Realism sees, when it has an honest purpose, as a form of love. In the same way as a wall may be washed because we care for the wall, so a person may be told he has welcomed something harmful to himself. Furthermore, if a person has begun to show something which represents him, we should hope that he believes more in this good sign.

All this arises from the need of a man to be as critical as he can be of things and persons in the whole world. Likewise he must encourage things and persons towards comeliness or aesthetic success. Man must see the flower well and the insect that may inimically visit the flower. When Blake, in a famous line of English poetry, said: "O Rose, thou art sick," he was aware of the possibilities of the rose.

Good will, then, instead of being a few words accompanying a handshake, is what we have when we are educated in the fullest way. The purpose of studying reality is to have good will for it. The Aesthetic Realism Consultation Trio, All For Education, with its beginning belief: "The purpose of education is to like the world," is saying that our study of the arts and sciences has, as its purpose, authentic good will for the world.

Contempt is a form of ill will, as both and anger and fear can be. Honest good will, wide in scope, various in presentation, specific as a petal, is the constant great enemy of contempt. So if contempt causes insanity, as I think it does and have said, good will is necessary if we are to lessen that imperfection or weakness of mind contempt makes for.

The Third Division, then of the study of Aesthetic Realism can be put this way:

III. Aesthetic Realism includes the study of good will as that which the human mind is aiming to have, for good will is a person's desire to see and increase the good meaning of all living beings and other realities.

4. What is Aesthetic Realism?

Bringing three divisions of Aesthetic Realism we have this:

Aesthetic Realism: A Study

    I.Aesthetic Realism, seeing contempt as the main cause of mental weakness and of insanity, studies contempt as something everyone is disposed to have as a means of strengthening himself and of lessening the meaning of reality.

II. Aesthetic Realism sees the world as the oneness of opposites, or aesthetics; and sees the oneness of opposites in the world as the one way of mitigating, lessening, and perhaps defeating the deep desire for contempt in everyone, with its accompanying mental weakening.

III. Aesthetic Realism includes the study of good will as that which the human mind is aiming to have, for good will is a person's desire to see and increase the good meaning of all living beings and other realities.

I have in this issue of TRO presented the three divisions of Aesthetic Realism. These divisions, like trees, may have ever so many branches, twigs, leaves; and relations among these. At the present time, life everywhere in the world is showing what these trees, branches, twigs, leaves of reality are; and what the relations of these are.

Reality, like art, is continuous and surprising. It is like a tree that has ingenuity and the possibility of entrancing and baffling. Indeed, one name of the tree is possibility.

With Love Eli Siegel

APPENDIX

There is no cure for herpes infection. There is not now a cure for herpes and there has never been a cure for herpes. In fact, until the drug Acyclovir came onto the market in 1985 (under the trade name Zovirax), there was no pharmaceutical treatment available for the treatment of herpes. Acyclovir itself provides no cure for herpes—when taken as directed and for the prescribed amount of time, Acyclovir simply suppresses outbreaks of the disease for long periods of time (keeping outbreaks effectively suppressed for months and even years and helping to control recurrent outbreaks once a chronic suppressive therapy has been discontinued).

This was my thinking going into calendar year 1995, when suit was brought against me in the state of Louisiana for suspension of my license to practice medicine. I had advertised in the Baton Rouge *Advocate* my practice at a clinic devoted to the treatment of genital herpes, using both Acyclovir and Aesthetic Realism as treatment modalities, which I announced, when used together, could effect a "complete remission" of herpes outbreaks. This was perhaps an unfortunate choice of words on my part, as the medical authorities of the state of Louisiana did proceed to suspend my license to practice there; but I never advertised an outright "cure" for herpes, nor did I make representations to that effect to any of those people that I treated in the course of my practice in this clinic. My words were seized upon with the intent of discrediting me, of marginalizing me, of relegating me to the trash heap, it seems to me, because the established medical community was (and continues to be) intimidated not by one of its own who has treated patients with an invaluable pharmaceutical agent but because I augmented that treatment with the teaching of Aesthetic Realism principles with my wife as a way of dealing with the underlying stress and psychological turmoil associated with the disease, stress which, if not dealt with effectively, can contribute to further painful outbreaks of the herpes infection.

It had become my position that Aesthetic Realism not only contributed to an easing of patients' stress levels but that, in conjunction with a chronic suppressive therapy using Acyclovir, patients could enjoy freedom from further outbreaks of this crippling disease. During the course of the proceedings, I arranged to have a deposition taken from Dr. Stanley M. Bierman, Clinical Professor of Medicine and Dermatology at UCLA. Dr. Bierman has spent over thirty years in medicine and has written about twenty papers dealing explicitly with herpes. He has chaired three national conferences on herpes and has taught courses at the American Academy of Dermatology on herpes simplex. He is, by all accounts and admissions, an acknowledged authority on the subject of herpes infections and its treatment.

In his deposition Dr. Bierman admitted how, back in the late 1970s, before Acyclovir had appeared as an effective treatment modality, he had been struck by the fact "that stress [in herpes sufferers] had a profound impact on host immunity." He recounted contacts he had had with Norman Cousins, whose own celebrated defense of positive mental and emotional attitudes in the face of threatening illnesses had given people reasons to suspect that patients' attitudes toward their disease were an important part of their receptivity to treatment and could even influence whether they took to a prescribed course of treatment when combatting a disease. Dr. Bierman had gone on to write and publish in the 1980s articles that dealt with the psychoneuroimmunological aspects of the effective treatment of herpes, in the conviction that the stress underlying and attending herpes infection would, if left untreated, contribute both to further outbreaks of herpes and to the severity of those outbreaks.

Dr. Bierman, when questioned about his treatment of herpes, spoke of cases that he had documented from the 1970s (prior to the availability of Acyclovir) of "protracted remission" (what others have referred to as "chronic remission"), by which he meant that herpes sufferers "would go from twelve attacks per year down to maybe one, or rare attacks lasting a brief period of time." Following the introduction of Acyclovir in 1985, and following initial clinical trials that lasted a year or less, it became clear to Dr. Bierman "that the drug would foreshorten the duration of infection but would not prevent recurrences." As evidence, he cited studies from the mid-1980s which showed that Acyclovir "effectively suppressed the disease in about eighty to ninety percent of cases. The problem was, when the drug was withdrawn and stopped, the patients, nearly one hundred percent, developed recurrences with the same frequency as before the drug was started." But successive and longer-term studies revealed that Acyclovir would effectively suppress herpes for months and years at a time.

Dr. Bierman routinely prescribed a two-year regimen of Acyclovir—one tablet three times a day for the first six months, one tablet twice a day for the second six months, and one tablet a day for the following year. For those following Dr.

Bierman's program, he reported that sixty to seventy percent of his patients would not experience recurrent outbreaks of herpes for up to two years following the end of the program. Patients would return to him periodically for treatment with Acyclovir when stress helped provoke a recurrent outbreak.

The upshot of Dr. Bierman's testimony was that Acyclovir by itself was a powerful agent for controlling outbreaks of herpes infection but that, all alone, it was closest to being 100% effective in suppressing recurrent herpes outbreaks only during the course of the two-year therapy program—once the program ended, patients were prone to recurrent outbreaks, particularly when they were overcome by stress. My approach, of course, was to treat not only the herpes infection pharmaceutically with Acyclovir but to treat underlying stress and patients' ability to cope with stress using the insights offered through the study of aesthetics and physiology.

Initial shock; emotional numbing; the frantic search for a cure; the sense of a profound isolation; a questioning of the durability of relationships; concerns over sexual gratification; anger directed against the source of the infection; fear of the consequences of herpes, in terms of communicability and childbirth; a general sense of fear, shame, and guilt; depression; helplessness; hopelessness; suicidal ideas; activation of any underlying psychopathology; disorganization of already inadequate coping mechanisms—this is a short catalogue of the purely psycho-social trauma that herpes sufferers go through, to one extent or another (not to mention the physical pain and disfigurement that so often accompany the disease). Acyclovir treats not a single one of these mental and emotional states. And any one of these reactions alone could give rise to significant levels of stress, stress that itself can easily trigger recurrent outbreaks of herpes, either when chronic suppressive Acyclovir therapy is not being used or when such a program has ended.

Dr. Bierman testified that, in the years before Acyclovir became available for the treatment of herpes, clinicians had used placebos effectively in treating patients with recurrent herpes outbreaks; the use of placebos such as sterile water reduced the frequency of recurrent outbreaks by some fifty to seventy percent (which is very suggestive of the important role that mental states play in the body's response to disease). Some clinical trials had involved the use of Lithium and of the antipsychotic drug Thorazine, and clinicians reported that "close to ninety percent of patients ... stopped having recurrences." These studies, too, point up the fact that patients' mental and emotional health had a highly significant role to play in the effective treatment of herpes, not to mention the huge role that mental and emotional equilibrium plays in someone's dealing with the stress that can aggravate recurrent outbreaks of herpes.

Close to half of Dr. Bierman's deposition concerned the abundant clinical literature and findings that stress is a major factor in triggering recurrent outbreaks of herpes. Much of the rest of the deposition concerned the semantical issue of what "remission" consists of and how it is distinguished from claims of a "cure" for herpes. Dr. Bierman's preferred term (as noted earlier) for the effective suppression of recurrent herpes outbreaks is "protracted remission" (the term I used in my advertisement, you may recall, was "complete remission," by which I meant a chronically suppressed herpes infection without incidence of recurrent outbreaks, which I maintain is both entirely possible and is the natural result of a therapy combining medication with Acyclovir and understanding of aesthetics and physiology). In his deposition Dr. Bierman went on to discuss the various perceptions of what "remission" consists of, in the eyes of healthcare professionals (including his own colleagues) and the general public (including some of his own patients). He stated clearly that no one in his experience had confused "remission" with "cure,' that "remission" was understood to mean a quiescent state of infection but not its complete and total eradication or elimination from the body. Dr. Bierman even allowed that the term "complete remission" could be used to characterize the period of effective suppression of recurrent outbreaks. (And now that I think about it, I can see how people tend not to be confused by what the term "remission" means because of its widespread use in therapies for treating various kinds of cancer—everyone knows that there's no cure for cancer, but most people understand what cancer "in remission" means.)

But Dr. Bierman"s testimony seems to have fallen on deaf ears, as the medical authorities of the state of Louisiana did proceed to suspend my license to practice there.

I'm not trying to plead my case there again. My license was suspended in Louisiana and I have no plans right now to go back there to practice. What I am trying to do in this book, though, is alert a vast public, a public that numbers millions of herpes sufferers, that there is hope in this dread affliction/that herpes infection does not mean the end of life as we know it, and that the infection can be effectively suppressed with a combined treatment of Acyclovir and the understanding of aesthetics and physiology. I'm not touting a "cure" for herpes— I'm only saying that the possibility exists for herpes sufferers to go through life free of recurrent outbreaks of herpes and that this possibility exists because of Acyclovir's ability to chronically suppress the herpes infection itself and because of Aesthetic Realism's ability to deal effectively with the underlying stress that can trigger recurrent herpes outbreaks.

Obviously, it is my claims concerning Aesthetic Realism, not my claims concerning Acyclovir, that have gotten me into trouble with the medical establishment. Many of "the powers that be" don't seem to want to admit to the usefulness of Aesthetic Realism or of any other alternative, "holistic" (in other words, non-pharmaceutical or non-surgical) procedure or therapy that produces solid results. All I can do, I suppose, is to teach what I learned helped me and to present my case to the people who are in a position to discover the truth for themselves, the millions in this country who are suffering from the physical and psychic disabilities of herpes.

*Dr. Okun holding baby daughter
Jane, April 1990.*

*I would like to express my gratitude to my wife,
Norma Okun, who has now authored "A Rose
Has Cried but Has Not Died" soon to be
published. A Rose Has Cried documents the
untoward and devastating removal of our
daughter, Jane and son Charlie from our care
due to Charlie's accusations of abuse lodged
against our relatives and their reaction to it,
soon after this photo was taken.*

Doctor Claims 'Aesthetic Realism' Saved Vision

By Susan Caslin
Town Talk Staff Writer

What a local doctor once termed "gobbledygook" has, he says, saved his vision. That "gobbledygook" will become the preventive medicine of the future, he says.

Dr. James D. Okun of Pineville and his wife, Norma, are gathering clinical research on Aesthetic Realism, a little-known philosophy applicable to preventive medicine.

They believe the relatively undiscovered philosophy can change the course of modern medicine and life.

The Okuns said AR has proven successful in the treatment of a variety of physical and mental conditions. Having been applied in cases of epilepsy, migraines, hypertension, ischemic heart disease and homosexuality, they hope to apply it further in dealing with such diseases as AIDS.

Okun was introduced to AR two years ago by his wife, an aesthetic consultant. Mrs. Okun began studying AR 16 years ago in New York under its founder, poet-author Eli Siegel. The couple now study cases of persons who successfully applied the philosophy to their lives and experienced changes in physical and mental health. Okun travels to New

York City for consultations with the AR Foundation.

From a doctor's point of view, AR provides perfect scientific criticism and analysis, Okun said. "That's what attracted me," he said. "I had all this scientific training and never had it applied in a way I could look at myself."

Okun, a 1978 graduate of Duke University, founded the Duke University Center for Tension Control in 1974 after becoming interested in the effect of stress on the body.

Sitting in his office Wednesday, he admits he had little faith in the philosophy until

(Turn to A-3)

White Collar Criminals

No Hasenfus Pardon,

★ 'Aesthetic Realism' Promoted

(Continued from Page 1)
it began to play a role in correcting his degenerative eye disease.

Four years ago, he was diagnosed with Keratoconus of the cornea, a disease which can lead to progressively worsening vision correctable only with rigid contract lenses.

"My vision in glasses was about non-existent and the vision with poorly fitting contact lenses was of such a low level that I would often get lost trying to find my own home," he says.

He decided to forgo the remaining two years of an opthalmology residency at Ochsner Foundation Hospital in New Orleans to seek medical help. He was advised by opthalmologists that his condition would remain the same or worsen, requiring one and possibly two corneal transplants.

After consultations with numerous doctors, he began to study AR two years ago. The study enabled him to relieve "deep psychological pain" linked to his vision problem and other aspects of his life, he said.

"As I continue(d) to study, it became apparent that my corneas were becoming flatter and flatter and my vision better and better," he says. "I became able to drive and work with good sight, not only in contact lenses but in glasses, which is unheard of in cases of keratoconus. Most recently, my corneas have become entirely normal with my vision crystal clear in contact lenses and in glasses."

He terms the improvement a "medical miracle" and believes it resulted from a release and lessening of internal stress and pain resulting from an "inaccurate and contemptuous way of seeing the world."

Aesthetic Realism, founded in the 1940's, is basically a way of seeing the world. It views reality, including oneself, as the aesthetic oneness of opposites: The world, art and self explain each other.

The complicated philosophy is comprised of four basic statements:

● Every person is trying to put together opposites in himself.

● Every person, in order to respect himself, has to see the world as beautiful or good or acceptable.

● There is a disposition in every person to think he will be for himself by making less of the outside world.

● All beauty is a making one of opposites, and that is what we seek in ourselves.

Norma Okun, a native of El Salvador, says AR reversed negative attitudes she held about herself, her native country and even her Spanish language.

AR teaches people a "more accurate way of coping" with reality, the couple explained. The Okuns have been invited to speak about the philosophy on Salvadoran national television to counsel people in that country in dealing with the aftermath of a major earthquake which struck San Salvador in October.

One's attitude towards things and people greatly affect the body, they point out. Stress has a direct impact on physical health, weakening the immunity system. AR is a method of studying and dealing with stress.

"If you don't do all you can to like the world, you will weaken yourself," Mrs. Okun said.

Contempt is a dangerous tendency, according to aesthetic realists. Persons who express contempt for things and people think they feel better by doing so. Aesthetic realists view such a tendency as the cause of insanity and general mental disorder.

"Aesthetic Realism makes the study of good will possible," Mrs. Okun said. "You can study how to have good will for another person."

It's a concept which has been around for years, but has never received widespread attention. "People would rather be superior to it than learn from it," Okun said.

As it becomes known, it will be tested further as to its effect on the body's immune system, Okun said.

"Eventually, it will be taught in medical schools," he predicted.

"Aesthetic Realism is not in competition with anything else," he said. "It's a beautiful adjunct to medicine, religion and any counseling, but it takes it one step further."

n, Justice Minister States

y he   and five other captives.
ar-   Obando y Bravo, who mediated
this possibility is open," he replied, and then added: "We have

N
O
V

227

ERASING SCARS

*Since the beginning of time pioneers in the field
of health have met violent opposition because
they threatened traditional medicine.I wish I
had known more when an article was published
in 1986 expressing my gratitude to Eli Siegel
and Aesthetic Realism as I subsequently lost my
livelihood and my only daughter and son. But, I
am proud forever to have met the truth.*

UofL Health Sciences Center

Department of Ophthalmology and Visual Sciences	University of Louisville School of Medicine	Kentucky Lions Eye Center 301 E. Muhammad Ali Blvd Louisville, Kentucky 40202-1594

November 22, 2004

Merian Glasper
Director Licensure
Louisiana State Board of Medical Licensure
630 Camp Street
New Orleans, LA 70130

RE: James D. Okun, M.D.

Dear Ms. Glasper:

Dr. James Okun was selected for a residency position in Ophthalmology at the Ochsner Medical Clinic in 1982 where I was Chairman of the department. His PGY-2 year began July 1984 and ended July 1985. Dr. Okun was Phi Beta Kappa at Duke University and had an outstanding medical school career at the Albert Einstein College of Medicine in New York. We put him at the very top of our match list and were extremely impressed with his abilities as an ophthalmology resident while at Ochsner. Unfortunately for us, he developed some mild corneal problems and decided to switch into emergency medicine after that resolved.

He was extremely well respected by his peers and by our staff physicians. He was especially well regarded for his fine quality work and care given in emergency situations while on call in-house at the Ear, Nose and Throat Hospital of New Orleans for his first four months and the emergency room at Ochsner after that.

James is highly intelligent, compassionate, and caring. I recommend him without reservation and he should certainly be given full credit for his year at Ochsner.

Sincerely,

Thom J. Zimmerman, M.D., Ph.D.
Emeritus Professor and Chairman
Department of Ophthalmology & Visual Sciences

Emeritus Professor of Pharmacology & Toxicology
University of Louisville
School of Medicine

Global Ophthalmic Medical Director
Pfizer, Inc.

Letter of Recommendation from Dr. Thom Zimmerman inventor of the Timoptic eye drop to treat Glaucoma.

DISCLAIMER

THIS PROGRAM DOES NOT CLAIM TO BE A CURE FOR
HERPES OR ANY OTHER DISEASE.

We are not advocating our program as a replacement or substitute for any medications that you may be on. This program is simply an extremely effective adjunct method that, if studied carefully and adhered to, can help to prevent outbreaks caused by the herpes virus.

The crucial part of this program is to understand what is leading to the outbreaks in your life. There is no magical cure to any disease.

We are not in competition with any medicine or currently accepted medical treatment and do not claim to be a replacement for these.

Method

The method of this program is to understand:

1. what the herpes virus is and how you got infected in the first place.

2. how the virus reproduces and causes outbreaks.

3. what the effect of this has been on your life both physically and psychologically.

4. with the above, to understand and be able to trace exactly what events or situations in your life or people you deal with actually trigger the outbreaks.

5. through brand new concepts, the makeup of your psychological self and how you are leading to and allowing your own illness.

6. through various assignments and study what you can do to deal with the same stimuli in a different way, to avoid using them to have an outbreak.

List of Assignments

Every time you have an outbreak, you are going to have to complete your outbreak log. You need to keep a record of the date when the blisters erupted, any symptoms you had before, like tingling or burning, redness or pain, how long the outbreak lasted, how long it took the blisters to crust over, whether you were taking any medications during the outbreak, and most importantly what you have gone through personally especially in the two weeks prior to the outbreak. What did you see as the major stresses in your life in the two weeks or more preceding the outbreak? Are there any people who you deal with in your life who:

A. make a lot out of you and compliment you, praise you, and make you feel very important?

B. insult you, put you down, make less of you, and make your life miserable?

C. are combinations of A and B and want to possess you in a bad way, want to manipulate you and have their way with you?

D. you may have had to deal with preceding your outbreak, who act like friends to your face and curse you or betray you to others behind your back.

Who is the stupidest person that you know?

Who is the person that makes you the angriest?

Do you have a hard time expressing yourself to them?

List what you like most about yourself and what you dislike most about yourself. Find one thing that you truly like in your day and write it down.

How many sides do you have, one side or two sides? Answer this after you have read the transcript.

After you have read the transcript, do you feel that there's something in you that wants to make less of people and hate them simply to boost yourself up, which may have a bad effect on your health?

Keep a log of 1) who has insulted you today and how you responded to it, and 2) who complimented you today. Keep a list.

E.   What was the worst thought of the day and the best thought, and who did you find yourself hating today? Do you feel stronger or weaker when you get around relatives, and do you have the respect that you should for them? Do you feel more lonely, sad or happy, and free most days? Do you feel like life is worth living, or would you rather be dead?

Write down the happiest day you can remember. Are you grateful for the things that you have, and would you do anything to be well, including being critical of yourself? Do you get furious when someone close to you tells you that you are not perfect?

Do you hate things or people that you cared about or who affected you just a few hours ago?

Is your health the most important thing that you have?

www.ingramcontent.com/pod-product-compliance
Lightning Source LLC
Chambersburg PA
CBHW072117020426
42334CB00018B/1628